Seven Windows

to

A Child's World

100 IDEAS FOR THE
MULTIPLE INTELLIGENCES CLASSROOM

By

Anna T. O'Connor

and

Sheila Callahan-Young

SkyLight

PROFESSIONAL DEVELOPMENT

Arlington Heights, Illinois

Seven Windows to a Child's World:
100 Ideas for the Multiple Intelligences Classroom

Published by SkyLight Professional Development
2626 S. Clearbrook Dr., Arlington Heights, Illinois 60005-5310
Phone 800-348-4474, 847-290-6600
Fax 847-290-6609
info@skylightedu.com
http://www.skylightedu.com

Creative Director: Robin Fogarty
Editors: Heidi Ray, Amy Wolgemuth, Julia Noblitt
Book Designer: Bruce Leckie
Illustration: David Stockman

Library of Congress Catalog Card Number: 94-78533
ISBN 0-932935-77-X
Printed in the United States of America

1252-V

Item Number 1261

Z Y X W V U T S R Q P O N M L K J I H G F E D C B A

06 05 04 03 02 01 00 99   15 14 13 12 11 10 9 8 7 6 5

DEDICATION

Dedicated to the "wonders in our lives":
Steve, Jason, Shelagh
and
Arthur

ACKNOWLEDGMENTS

We would like to acknowledge the contribution of many people for their encouragement, input, and expertise. We are grateful for their support and friendship. Thank you, Sally Bradshaw, Bill Bruns, Pam Card, Julie Carter, Ron Eckle, Dr. William Leary, Carol Lewis, Anthony Marino, Brian McKee, and Alyce McMenimen.

We give special thanks to Dr. Howard Gardner and Mara Krechevsky and the staff at Project Zero, Harvard University, for inspiring us to discover our strengths as teachers and learners.

We would like to thank our families for their patience and support. We could not have done this without you!

A NOTE FROM HOWARD GARDNER

Multiple intelligences are best cultivated when children become deeply involved with intriguing materials and have the opportunity to draw naturally and appropriately on their several intelligences. Based on several years of experimentation in their classrooms, Anna O'Connor and Sheila Callahan-Young have assembled an inviting set of materials and exercises which can enrich the lives and heighten the productivity of children everywhere.

Howard Gardner
Harvard Project Zero
1994

Grateful acknowledgment is made to the following publishers for their permission to reprint copyrighted material.

Ira Sleeps Over by Bernard Waber is used with permission of Houghton Mifflin Company, Boston. Copyright © 1972, Houghton Mifflin.

Alexander and the Terrible, Horrible, No Good, Very Bad Day by Judith Viorst is used with permission of Macmillan Publishing Company, New York. Copyright © 1972, Macmillan.

It Didn't Frighten Me! by Janet Goss and Jerome Harste is used with permission of Willowisp Press, St. Petersburg, Fla. Copyright © 1985, Willowisp Press.

The Snowy Day by Ezra Jack Keats is used with permission of Penguin USA, New York. Copyright © 1962, Penguin.

The Jacket I Wear in the Snow by Shirley Neitzel is used with permission of William Morrow Company. Copyright © 1989, William Morrow.

"The Little Prince" is used with permission of Silver Burdett Company. Copyright © 1964, 1965, Silver Burdett.

Contents

UNIT 2: FALL 53
Outline 54
Vocabulary 57

Lesson Plans

UNIT 3:   DAY/NIGHT   107
Outline   108
Vocabulary   110

Lesson Plans

ix

UNIT 4: WINTER 157

Outline 158

Vocabulary 160

Lesson Plans

CONTENTS

UNIT 5:   CASTLES   207
Outline   208
Vocabulary   210

Lesson Plans

Introduction

INCLUDING MULTIPLE INTELLIGENCES IN THE CURRICULUM

Many Kindergarten and Primary curriculum guides are available to assist teachers in providing a well-rounded program for four-, five-, six-, and seven-year-olds. This guide, however, is the first, to our knowledge, to focus specifically on multiple intelligences in the classroom.

For the last four years, we have studied the development and evaluation of curriculum using Gardner's Multiple Intelligences theory. Dr. Gardner, Harvard psychologist and author of *Frames of Mind* (HarperCollins, 1983), asserts that seven areas of "intelligence" characterize human beings. The traditional school has focused mainly on math and linguistic skills but Gardner suggests that there are at least five other ways of knowing. He has identified seven intelligences, though he admits there may be more. They include linguistic, logical-mathematical, spatial, bodily-kinesthetic, musical, interpersonal, and intrapersonal. The linguistic intelligence involves the production of language including writing, poetry, and storytelling. The logical-mathematical intelligence involves problem solving, inductive and deductive thinking, working with symbols, and recognizing patterns. The spatial intelligence involves both the visual arts (painting and sculpture) and assembly (how things work, come apart, and are put together). The bodily-kinesthetic intelligence involves the ability to use the body to play games and to express emotion. The musical intelligence involves recognizing tones and sensitivity to vocal, instrumental, and environmental sounds. The interpersonal intelligence includes the ability to work well with others. The intrapersonal intelligence involves self-knowledge, metacognition, and self-reflection.

In our primary multiple intelligence curriculum we have chosen to combine the interpersonal and intrapersonal intelligences as integral parts of each social lesson. The reason for this union is multipurpose.

At a young age, children explore their social parameters and discover who they are as individuals and as members of their peer group. A kindergarten or pre-kindergarten experience is often the initial opportunity for a child to be part of a large group. Some children come to school with a well-established sense of self and are able to observe others and understand the motivation behind peer interaction. But many children have received little guidance in self-responsibility and are barely aware of their own motivations and actions and often do not understand consequences.

Howard Gardner describes the interpersonal and intrapersonal intelligences as the "personal intelligences." These intelligences encompass human feelings. In our interpretation of Gardner's theory, we find the transition from the theoretical to the practical more difficult in the case of the intrapersonal and interpersonal intelligences. These two intelligences lack the concrete qualities necessary to shift from the current educational curriculum to a multiple intelligences curriculum.

We have chosen, therefore, to enhance traditional primary lessons aimed at developing social skills among young children by including self-reflection—asking the child to look inward for self perceptions—and observation—asking the child to look outward to perceive distinctions among others. In this way, the students' personal strengths emerge. The classroom teacher understands the difference between the interpersonal and intrapersonal intelligences through the use of guiding questions and through observation.

It is our contention that any type of lesson may include social (interpersonal and intrapersonal) elements by including pertinent self-reflection and observation within the structure of the lesson. However, a primarily social lesson poses a problem or situation that requires an inward or outward examination.

Gardner's spatial intelligence comprises a mixture of abilities exemplified by recreating one's visual experiences. We have found different aspects of the spatial intelligence to be of more or less interest to a child, often in correlation with the child's level of fine motor development. We have observed primary children who struggle or frustrate easily with an artistic task, but enthusiastically devote time and attention to three-dimensional constructions or vice versa. In light of this observation we chose to include both artistic and assembly tasks as important components of the spatial intelligence.

Traditional primary classrooms often provide fewer opportunities for problem solving through assembly tasks as children grow older. Our observations of Kindergartners led us to conclude that assembly tasks enhance the development of fine motor skills, self-esteem, and problem-solving abilities. Children often choose spatial/assembly tasks as their favorite. Despite their limited assembly ability, young children describe their experiences as successful. The feeling of success stems from the perception that a construction is never wrong—errors can be reworked and changed because of the flexible nature of the materials. In contrast, despite emphasis on process with spatial/artistic tasks, children are more likely to be unhappy with their end product because they are unable to execute the visual experience they desire to recreate.

To encourage learning in the spatial intelligence, each thematic unit comprises three spatial/assembly lessons and three spatial/artistic lessons. At all levels, the value of construction tasks needs to be honored and emphasized in the curriculum. Although hands-on tasks are usually included in the traditional curriculum, we have included specific spatial lessons to accentuate their value and necessity.

ABOUT THIS CURRICULUM GUIDE

This curriculum guide is the result of applying Gardner's theory in our Kindergarten classes. It provides teachers with a practical hands-on approach to instruction—a teacher-friendly program easily adapted to any primary classroom. The lesson plans provide a model for teachers who wish to develop multiple intelligences units in other areas of interest.

Each unit comprises twenty-one lessons designed to challenge children's thinking in the seven areas of intelligence. Lessons incorporate whole group, small group, and learning centers. Specific trade materials familiar to most teachers are suggested for many lessons, but teachers can adapt these lessons using their available resources.

A few lessons include homework designed to strengthen the communication between home and school. Parents are encouraged to view and give feedback for projects completed in school, to help extend a lesson begun in school, and to reinforce skills taught in school. We have found that many parents appreciate being included in their child's school life through homework assignments.

Some lessons include designated portfolio samples with format suggestions for collection throughout the school year. Each unit includes seven portfolio suggestions, one for each area of intelligence. These samples have been thoughtfully chosen to meet our assessment needs. Classroom teachers may use our suggestions or may designate other lessons more suitable for their specific needs.

We have suggested varied formats for recording examples of children's learning. Anecdotal records include teacher-made forms, checklists, and narratives. Performance samples of art, math, and construction can be collected through work samples, artifacts, and photographs. Audiotape and videotape can be used to record musical, social, linguistic, and movement behaviors. We suggest these sample performances be collected over time, so that they may become representative examples of growth and change.

Portfolio samples are examples of individual as well as whole group performances. A large group of visual artwork samples, for example, is compared to establish standards from superior to below average performance in the spatial/artistic intelligence. In the same way, whole class videotapes of movement lessons are examined to determine ranges in bodily-kinesthetic abilities.

Our major objective is to help children develop skills necessary to become productive members of their community. The curriculum focuses on children's unique traits and their commonalities. Thematic learning encourages children to explore themselves and their environment in a variety of meaningful ways. We feel that the lessons developed here help children make conscious decisions, thereby increasing their self-awareness. Opportunities are provided for creative expression and detailed investigation in all areas of intelligence. These areas of strength and interest may be used by the teacher as "entry points" into skill areas that are more difficult for the child. Through exposure and exploration, children with strengths in non-traditional intelligence areas are given the opportunity to succeed.

HOW TO USE THIS BOOK

Each unit includes three lessons for each of the seven intelligences. Each lesson requires approximately thirty minutes except where noted. In many cases children will desire more time to fully explore special interests. To allow for further investigations, make materials available at learning centers during choice times throughout each week. Additional thematic lessons are left to the discretion of each classroom teacher who is most familiar with the needs and interests of his or her students.

Some lessons incorporate stories and songs from other sources. Bibliographic information for these stories and songs is included at the end of each unit.

This curriculum views the teacher as facilitator. When the teacher takes an active role, stimulating creativity by asking thought-provoking questions, creative, divergent ideas are likely to be evoked. Divergent thinking is elicited by asking questions like these: "What could you (we) do? What else could you (we) do? I wonder if there is another way? What do you think?" Thought-provoking questions emphasize process and problem solving and inspire multiple solutions and answers. Using the inquiry method invites children to think.

The teacher's responsibility includes not only guidance, to coach the child as she or he engages in activities, but also acceptance. The teacher creates an environment in which the child is encouraged to put ideas into practice, to investigate, and to discover meaning for him- or herself. The teacher's attitudes determine the classroom climate and are the keys to building positive and realistic self-images in the child. The teacher who shares descriptive and non-judgmental reactions to the child's work through personal interaction enhances a positive self-concept. Discussing the creative details of the child's work with him or her validates and affirms the child's sense of self-esteem.

Self

This unit, Self, focuses on the child's introduction to school.

OBJECTIVES

- To understand that I am special and capable
- To know that I am accepted and valued as an individual and as part of a group
- To develop self-knowledge
- To enjoy school

1

SELF UNIT OUTLINE

 ## LINGUISTIC

Look What I Have   Children describe objects by color in a repetitive question-and-answer game.

Our Families   Children talk about their families, then create labeled family portraits.

Telephone Talk   Children role-play telephone conversations, practice their phone numbers, and have a surprise snack.

 ## LOGICAL-MATHEMATICAL

Graphing Eye Color   Observations about eyes lead to a class graph full of revealing information.

Exploration of Math Manipulatives   Children are introduced to a variety of math materials.

People Patterns   Personal attributes of classmates are used to create patterns.

 ## SPATIAL/ARTISTIC

Paper Plate Faces   Children discuss symmetry, then create their own likeness on a paper plate.

Class Quilts   Full-body self portraits are mounted on craft paper to create a class quilt.

Fabulous Fingers and Hands   Primary colors are explored with finger paints.

INTER- AND INTRAPERSONAL/SOCIAL

All by Myself   Children listen to a story about self-knowledge and discuss and draw what they and others are capable of doing independently.

Our Unique Faces   Children reflect on their own unique image, then create their own likeness.

I Was Mad   Children listen to a story about feelings and describe and draw pictures of their own angry feelings.

SPATIAL/ASSEMBLY

Block Building   Children use blocks to build a structure to play inside.

Familiar Fun Building   Children explore a variety of construction manipulatives.

Puzzle Play   Children share strategies for completing puzzles.

BODILY-KINESTHETIC

Finding Your Personal Space   Children make discoveries about personal or "home" space and explore movement with their hands.

Aerobic Exercise   Children are introduced to aerobic exercise and take turns leading the group.

Make Your Move   Children explore movement in a variety of ways and use different parts of their bodies to move fast and slow.

MUSICAL

Your Body Keeps the Beat   A song, rhyme, game, and chant introduce keeping the beat to the children.

You Can Play the Drum   Children explore keeping the beat with a hand drum and experiment with pitch and affect through singing.

Percussion Instrument Families   A rhyme introduces instrument families and children classify instruments by sound quality.

VOCABULARY

This vocabulary list includes language that is used in the lessons for this unit. At the beginning of a lesson you can introduce key words and ask the children to define them and present materials for labeling. Language that you have introduced and that children have generated is used throughout a lesson. After a lesson, let children re-evaluate their definitions and clarify meaning for themselves.

address	high	special
aerobic	home	symmetry
alike	jingle	tempo
angry	left	Unifix cubes
answering machine	like	unique
art medium	loud	weight
balance	love	
beat	low	
body parts	mad	
change	patchen	
click	pattern	
clues	pattern blocks	
color names	percussion	
compare	personal space	
Cuissinaire rods	pitch	
different	portrait	
eye dropper	predict	
experiment	primary colors	
familiar	rattle	
family members	right	
fast	ring	
favorite	rotary dial	
features	sad	
feelings	same	
graph	scared	
grow	scrape	
hand drum	shape names	
happy	sibling	
hate	slow	
height	soft	

Unit: Self
Lesson Plans

Intelligence
Linguistic

1

Look What I Have

PROCEDURE

Read the story and discuss. Let each child choose one toy from the collection. Let children know that they will be using the name of their object and its color such as "blue fish." Sitting in a circle, each child tells the children on either side of her what she has chosen. To begin the game, the teacher says "Mrs. Smith, Mrs. Smith, what do you have?" The teacher responds: "I have a _____ sitting with me." All use the next person's name to ask, "___, ___, what do you have?" That person answers, "I have a _____ sitting with me." Questions and answers continue around the circle until everyone has had a turn.

GUIDING QUESTIONS

- What do you think this story will be about?
- How could we use this collection of toys to play a game?
- How would you describe the toy you have chosen?

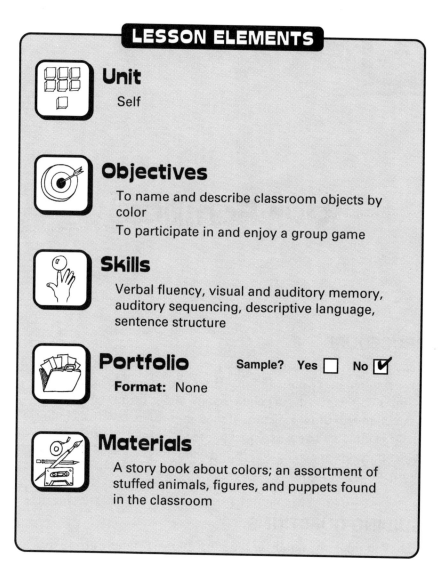

LESSON ELEMENTS

Unit
Self

Objectives
To name and describe classroom objects by color

To participate in and enjoy a group game

Skills
Verbal fluency, visual and auditory memory, auditory sequencing, descriptive language, sentence structure

Portfolio
Sample? Yes ☐ No ☑

Format: None

Materials
A story book about colors; an assortment of stuffed animals, figures, and puppets found in the classroom

COMMENTS

Children may choose to describe their toys in additional ways besides color (e.g., "silly green frog").

Once children know the game, the teacher or a child writes the name of one toy on a secret piece of paper. The person who chooses that toy begins the game. Let each child name toys in the circle at random. After playing, let children hide their toys and ask who remembers which toys each child had.

Intelligence
Linguistic

Our Families

PROCEDURE

Read the story and discuss. Display examples of family portraits and have children make observations. Discuss why people have family pictures on their walls. Let children talk about their own families. Ask children to draw a picture of their immediate family including pets. Let children choose colored paper to "frame" their portraits. When portraits are complete, record children's comments and label family members in their pictures.

GUIDING QUESTIONS

- Do you think the family in the story and your family are alike? Why or why not?
- How is your family different from this family?
- What would you like to tell us about your family?

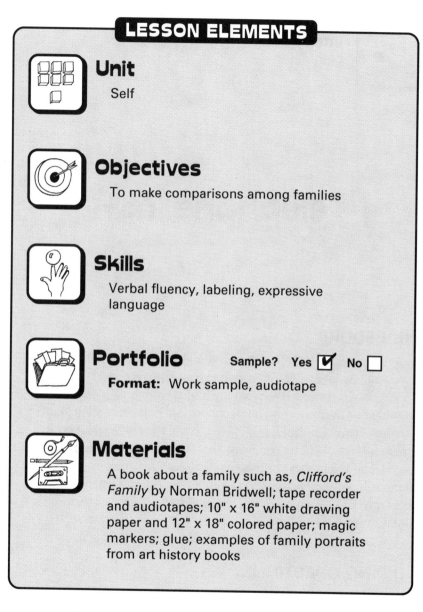

LESSON ELEMENTS

Unit
Self

Objectives
To make comparisons among families

Skills
Verbal fluency, labeling, expressive language

Portfolio
Sample? Yes ☑ No ☐

Format: Work sample, audiotape

Materials
A book about a family such as, *Clifford's Family* by Norman Bridwell; tape recorder and audiotapes; 10" x 16" white drawing paper and 12" x 18" colored paper; magic markers; glue; examples of family portraits from art history books

COMMENTS

This lesson could run longer than a thirty-minute time frame depending on the size of the group. Display family portraits prominently and discuss how classes of students are like families. Record children's responses on one audiotape.

Intelligence
Linguistic

Telephone Talk

PROCEDURE

Model answering the telephone and making calls, including leaving a message on an answering machine (use tape recorder). Discuss important skills needed for making and receiving calls. Ask for volunteers. Give one child a telephone. Use that child's telephone number, "call" the child, and have a conversation. Repeat with other children. Let one child call another. After modeling examples, use telephone number cards to pair children for conversations. Let some children use bananas as telephone receivers. In pairs children take turns calling each other. Have children talk about their conversations.

GUIDING QUESTIONS

- What are some important things to remember when using the telephone?
- What could you do if you didn't have a telephone or if your telephone was broken?

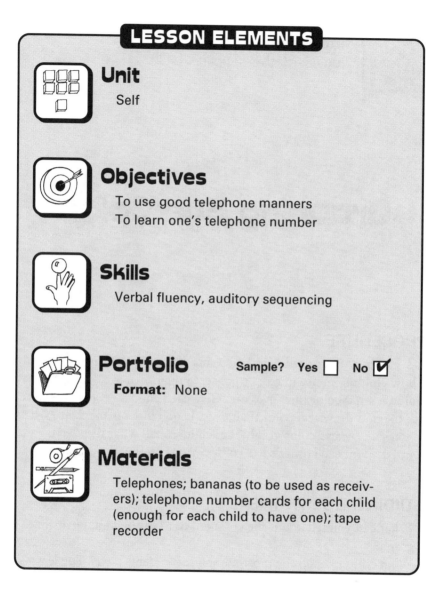

LESSON ELEMENTS

Unit
Self

Objectives
To use good telephone manners
To learn one's telephone number

Skills
Verbal fluency, auditory sequencing

Portfolio
Format: None

Sample? Yes ☐ No ☑

Materials
Telephones; bananas (to be used as receivers); telephone number cards for each child (enough for each child to have one); tape recorder

COMMENTS

After the lesson, eat the bananas for a snack.

Let children decide how to color code the function buttons of a tape recorder for their use. Set up a message machine center and allow children to tape-record messages to the teacher and/or peers on the "answering machine."

Intelligence
Logical-Mathematical

Graphing Eye Color

PROCEDURE

Ask children to work in pairs observing each other's eye color.
Allow children to use mirrors to observe their own eye color. Ask
children what color their eyes are. Give each child a Post-it note and
ask them to draw and color their eyes. Let children place their Post-
it notes on the eye color graph. Let children tell what they have
learned about each other's eye color by interpreting the graph.

GUIDING QUESTIONS

- What can you tell about the colors of our eyes by looking at the
  graph?
- What color eyes do the most number of students have? The least
  number?
- How many more children have (brown) eyes than (blue) eyes?
- What other information could we graph besides eye color? How?

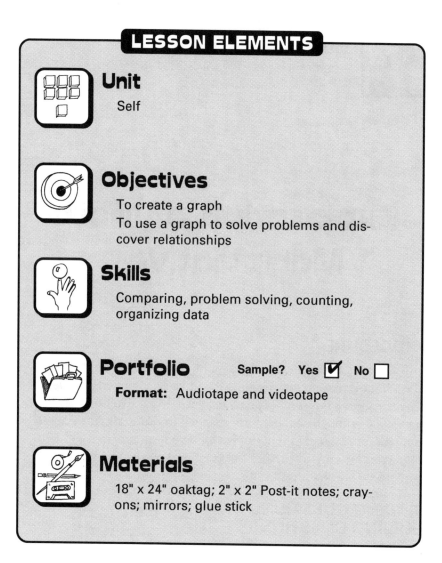

LESSON ELEMENTS

Unit
Self

Objectives
To create a graph
To use a graph to solve problems and discover relationships

Skills
Comparing, problem solving, counting, organizing data

Portfolio
Sample? Yes ☑ No ☐
Format: Audiotape and videotape

Materials
18" x 24" oaktag; 2" x 2" Post-it notes; crayons; mirrors; glue stick

COMMENTS

To create the graph, write the question, "What color are your eyes?" across the top of a piece of oaktag. Let children name all the different eye colors. Draw or write "blue eyes," "brown eyes," "green eyes," etc. as column headings under the question. Have children take turns placing their Post-it notes in the correct column.

Intelligence
Logical-Mathematical

Exploration of Math Manipulatives

PROCEDURE

Introduce the materials by asking children if they know the names of each. Let children make suggestions for the use of each material. Divide children into four groups. Let each group explore their materials. While the children are engaged in exploration, circulate among groups asking thought-provoking questions. Give children ample opportunity to explore each material. Make the materials available at the math center for free exploration.

GUIDING QUESTIONS

- How many different ways can you fill a large container with rice?
- How could you use these Unifix™ cubes?
- What are the least number of sides on a pattern block? the most number of sides?
- What have you noticed about the length of these rods?

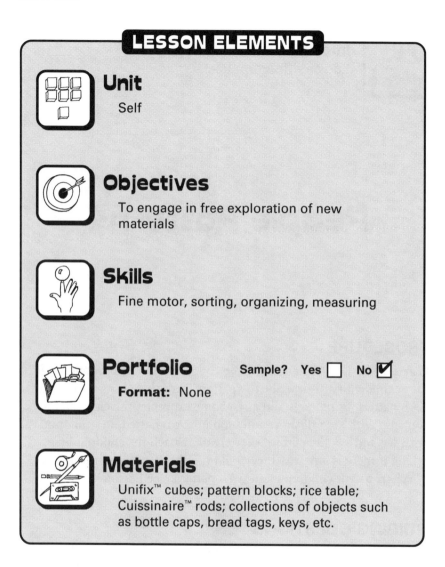

LESSON ELEMENTS

Unit

Self

Objectives

To engage in free exploration of new materials

Skills

Fine motor, sorting, organizing, measuring

Portfolio   Sample? Yes ☐ No ☑

Format: None

Materials

Unifix™ cubes; pattern blocks; rice table; Cuissinaire™ rods; collections of objects such as bottle caps, bread tags, keys, etc.

COMMENTS

Children need to know that materials such as rice must be handled carefully and kept in the rice table. As children are exploring, the teacher makes observations such as who explores by ordering, sorting, or organizing, who generates ideas easily, who prefers to work alone, who prefers to work with others, etc.

Intelligence
Logical-Mathematical

People Patterns

PROCEDURE

Clap a pattern (AAB) and have the children join in. Ask children if they can identify or describe the pattern. Ask them how to make an AAB pattern using boys and girls. Some examples the children might come up with are tall/short and blond/brown haired. Let children both see and say the pattern they create. Coach the children by asking if there is any way they could use the information from their eye chart to put children in an AAB pattern (see Lesson 4).

GUIDING QUESTIONS

- What are other ways we can use people in our class to make patterns?
- What other patterns could we make?
- Have you noticed any patterns in our classroom? What are they? Can you show us how you would clap that pattern? Could you make that pattern using boys and girls?

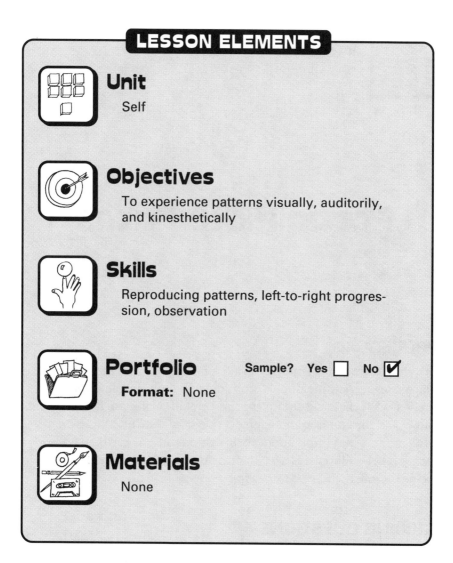

LESSON ELEMENTS

Unit
Self

Objectives
To experience patterns visually, auditorily, and kinesthetically

Skills
Reproducing patterns, left-to-right progression, observation

Portfolio
Sample? Yes ☐ No ☑

Format: None

Materials
None

COMMENTS
Children will be familiar with patterns from calendar experiences in their classrooms.

Intelligence
Spatial/Artistic

Paper Plate Faces

PROCEDURE

Begin by discussing symmetry using a facial photograph from a magazine. Present the photograph folded in half. Let children predict what they will see on the hidden half. Compare the two sides. Ask the children to imagine a line down the middle of their faces and think about their features and where they are located. Let children describe their features including the position, shape, number, and color of each.

GUIDING QUESTIONS

- What does your face look like?
- Can you look at a friend and tell us everything you see on your friend's face?
- How could you use these materials to make a face that looks like yours?

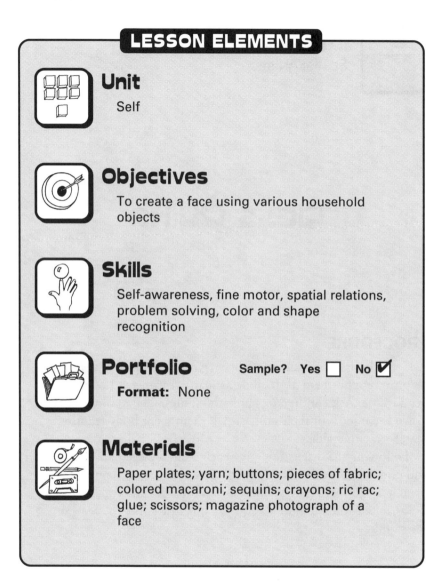

LESSON ELEMENTS

Unit
Self

Objectives
To create a face using various household objects

Skills
Self-awareness, fine motor, spatial relations, problem solving, color and shape recognition

Portfolio
Sample? Yes ☐ No ☑

Format: None

Materials
Paper plates; yarn; buttons; pieces of fabric; colored macaroni; sequins; crayons; ric rac; glue; scissors; magazine photograph of a face

COMMENTS

Each child is given a plate and chooses objects that resemble facial features to make his or her own face. These objects are arranged on the plate first and then glued in place.

Intelligence
Spatial/Artistic

Class Quilts

PROCEDURE

Ask the children to name some body parts. Ask what shapes these features remind them of. Include as many features as possible from head to toe. Ask children to think about an imaginary line drawn down the middle of their bodies. Ask them what body features match on either side.

Following the discussion, give each child a piece of 9" x 9" paper and crayons. Ask them to draw a whole picture of themselves from head to toe. Let the children sign the bottom of their drawings if possible. Mount children's squares on craft paper to create a class quilt.

GUIDING QUESTIONS

- How do you and your friends look alike?
- How do you look different from your friends?
- What parts are most important to include in a picture of yourself?

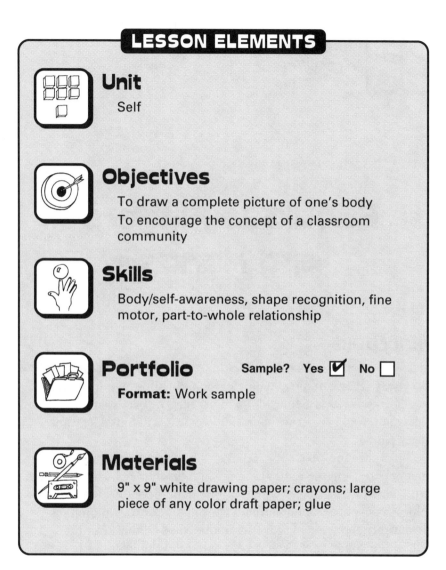

LESSON ELEMENTS

Unit
Self

Objectives
To draw a complete picture of one's body
To encourage the concept of a classroom
community

Skills
Body/self-awareness, shape recognition, fine
motor, part-to-whole relationship

Portfolio
Sample? Yes ☑ No ☐
Format: Work sample

Materials
9" x 9" white drawing paper; crayons; large
piece of any color draft paper; glue

COMMENTS
You may wish to introduce self-portraits by familiarizing children
with the work of well-known master artists.

Intelligence
Spatial/Artistic

Fabulous Fingers and Hands

PROCEDURE

Give each child a piece of finger-paint paper. Ask the children to show ways they can move their fingers and hands on paper (wiggle, hold stiff, scratch, use knuckles, palms, sides of hands, etc.). Ask children to predict what each movement will look like using finger paint.

Encourage multiple approaches and unusual ideas. Put water on each paper; using the right amount is important. Each child selects two colors to experiment with. Put one tablespoon of each chosen color on the paper. Let children have ample time to explore their movements and make discoveries about color mixing. Ask the children to compare their new colors and their predictions to the end results.

GUIDING QUESTIONS

- What are some ways you can move your fingers and hands?
- What do you think is going to happen when you mix your two colors?

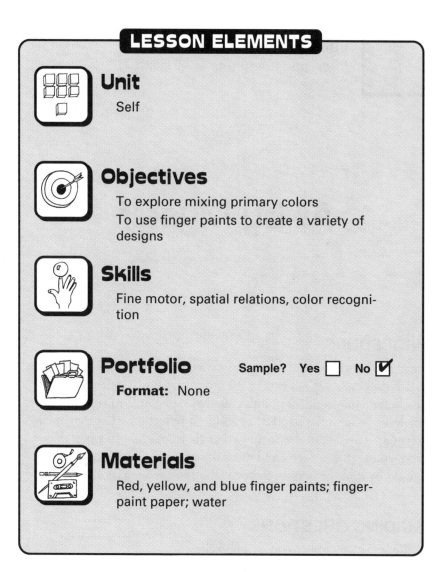

LESSON ELEMENTS

Unit
Self

Objectives
To explore mixing primary colors
To use finger paints to create a variety of designs

Skills
Fine motor, spatial relations, color recognition

Portfolio
Sample? Yes ☐ No ☑
Format: None

Materials
Red, yellow, and blue finger paints; finger-paint paper; water

COMMENTS
The teacher should experiment with water and paint prior to the lesson.

Intelligence
Inter- and Intrapersonal/Social

All by Myself

PROCEDURE

Read the suggested story or a story with characters that children can relate to. Discuss the events in the story that illustrate the character's independent abilities such as being able to ride a bike or wash his or her own hands. Let children reflect on what they themselves are capable of doing now, that they couldn't do when they were younger. Let each child draw a picture of something he or she can do by him- or herself. Record children's explanations.

GUIDING QUESTIONS

- What are you able to do by yourself?
- Why do you suppose you are able to ___?
- What have you noticed that others can do by themselves?

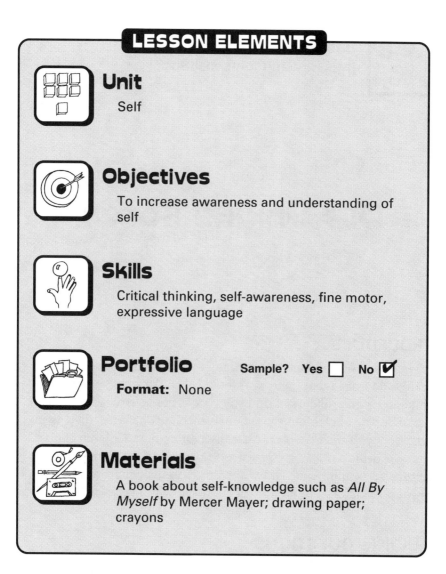

LESSON ELEMENTS

Unit
Self

Objectives
To increase awareness and understanding of self

Skills
Critical thinking, self-awareness, fine motor, expressive language

Portfolio
Sample? Yes ☐ No ☑

Format: None

Materials
A book about self-knowledge such as *All By Myself* by Mercer Mayer; drawing paper; crayons

COMMENTS

You may want to look at other books featuring independent characters that children can relate to. Children may want to compare abilities of children of different ages.

Intelligence
Inter- and Intrapersonal/Social

11

Our Unique Faces

PROCEDURE

Begin with guided imagery (see page 28). After the story, ask children to describe what their faces look like to them. In pairs let children identify likenesses and compare differences with each other. Let each pair of children share one likeness or difference they have observed with their partner. After discussion, have children choose a circle or oval to trace on construction paper and draw their facial features. Ask children to draw themselves as accurately as possible. Encourage children to use mirrors to assist with likenesses.

GUIDING QUESTIONS

- How is your face different from other faces in our class?
- How is your face the same as other faces in our class?
- What have you noticed about the faces of your friends?

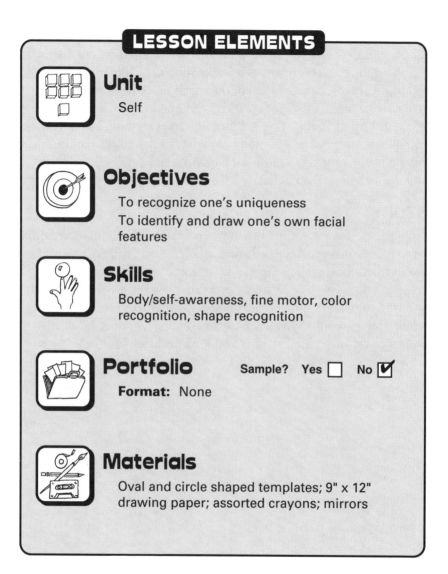

LESSON ELEMENTS

Unit
Self

Objectives
To recognize one's uniqueness
To identify and draw one's own facial features

Skills
Body/self-awareness, fine motor, color recognition, shape recognition

Portfolio
Sample? Yes ☐ No ☑
Format: None

Materials
Oval and circle shaped templates; 9" x 12" drawing paper; assorted crayons; mirrors

COMMENTS
The teacher models tracing, but some children will need assistance with this task.

(Lesson continued on the next page.)

GUIDED IMAGERY

Close your eyes and take a deep breath. While inhaling say "Breathing in, in, in," several times. While exhaling say, "Breathing out, out, out" several times. Take another deep breath and repeat this sequence two more times. Say, "You feel good inside. You are relaxed. You are quiet. You are listening to everything I say. You are listening to my words. You will hear what I say and see pictures in your mind." Take three more deep breaths and say, "Get comfortable for the story I am going to tell you."

STORY

"Imagine you are in a safe, warm place. Imagine a mirror, a very large mirror in a sparkling yellow frame. Imagine you see yourself in the mirror. Look at your face; look at the color of your hair, the color of your eyes; wiggle your nose; show your shiny white teeth. Smile at yourself in the mirror. Look at your whole face. Your whole face is smiling, you are happy and you feel good. Look at your face again, remember how you look and feel."

UNIT: SELF

Intelligence
Inter- and Intrapersonal/Social

I Was Mad

PROCEDURE

Read a story that focuses on the recognition of feelings. Let children talk about familiar experiences that make them feel mad. Let children describe their angry feelings and behaviors. Ask children to draw pictures of what makes them mad and label pictures, "It makes me so mad when. . . ." Document children's responses. Bind pictures into a class big book.

GUIDING QUESTIONS

- What makes you feel mad (sad, happy, tired, angry)? Why?
- How do you know when your friends are angry? sad? happy?
- Why do you suppose they feel that way?

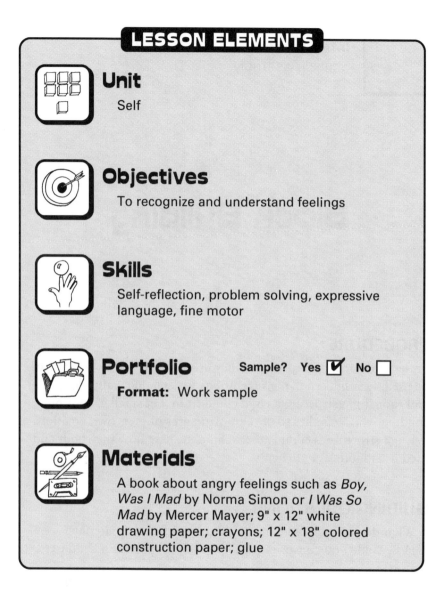

LESSON ELEMENTS

Unit
Self

Objectives
To recognize and understand feelings

Skills
Self-reflection, problem solving, expressive language, fine motor

Portfolio
Sample? Yes ☑ No ☐

Format: Work sample

Materials
A book about angry feelings such as *Boy, Was I Mad* by Norma Simon or *I Was So Mad* by Mercer Mayer; 9" x 12" white drawing paper; crayons; 12" x 18" colored construction paper; glue

COMMENTS

Provide a social area with paper and markers. Children can draw pictures that depict emotions—sad, happy, angry—and create cards to play charades with their peers.

Intelligence
Spatial/Assembly

Block Building

PROCEDURE

Present materials. Discuss what they are made of and how they can be used. Let children make suggestions for creating walls, doors, and roofs for a structure a child could fit in. Let small groups of children work together to develop structures of their own creation. When a structure is complete, let children share how they built and used it with others in the class.

GUIDING QUESTIONS

- What do you suppose you could build with these materials?
- How could you construct a building big enough for a child to fit inside?
- What part of your structure was easiest for you? hardest? Why?
- How would you change the structure?

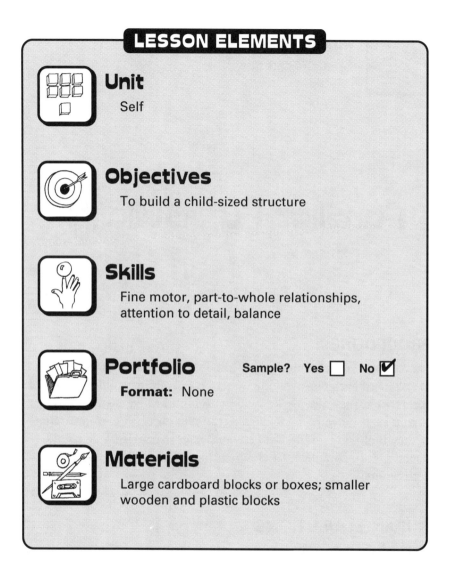

LESSON ELEMENTS

Unit
Self

Objectives
To build a child-sized structure

Skills
Fine motor, part-to-whole relationships, attention to detail, balance

Portfolio
Sample? Yes ☐ No ☑

Format: None

Materials
Large cardboard blocks or boxes; smaller wooden and plastic blocks

COMMENTS

Children like to have their finished structures photographed. At that time, they can tell about the problems they encountered and the discoveries they made.

33

Intelligence
Spatial/Assembly

Familiar Fun Building

PROCEDURE

Let children tell what they know about using the materials. Discuss the name of each construction material. Encourage children to show others what they already know how to build. Make instructions or examples displayed on packaging available for children to examine as they build. Let children try to build new structures. When constructions are complete, let children share their building strategies with others.

GUIDING QUESTIONS

- How have you used these materials in the past?
- What new structures would you like to build?
- How did you assemble that structure?

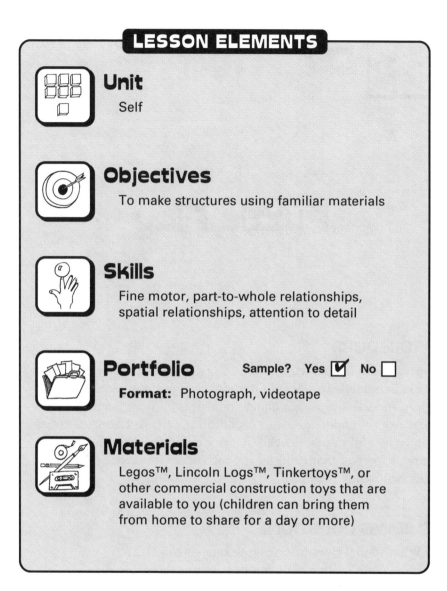

LESSON ELEMENTS

Unit
Self

Objectives
To make structures using familiar materials

Skills
Fine motor, part-to-whole relationships, spatial relationships, attention to detail

Portfolio
Sample? Yes ☑ No ☐

Format: Photograph, videotape

Materials
Legos™, Lincoln Logs™, Tinkertoys™, or other commercial construction toys that are available to you (children can bring them from home to share for a day or more)

COMMENTS

Children can be photographed with their structures or videotaped explaining how they built their structures.

35

Intelligence
Spatial/Assembly

Puzzle Play

PROCEDURE

Display a framed tabletop puzzle. Take pieces out randomly. Ask the children how they would begin to complete this puzzle, noting edges and color or design matching. Display a floor puzzle and its box. Ask the children how to begin this puzzle. Ask how the cover can be helpful. Allow the children free exploration time with the puzzles. Suggest that children ask each other for help first before seeking teacher assistance.

GUIDING QUESTIONS

- What special clues help you put puzzles together?
- Can you tell us how you put puzzles together?
- How can the frame of the puzzle help you?
- How can the colors and shapes of the puzzle pieces help you?

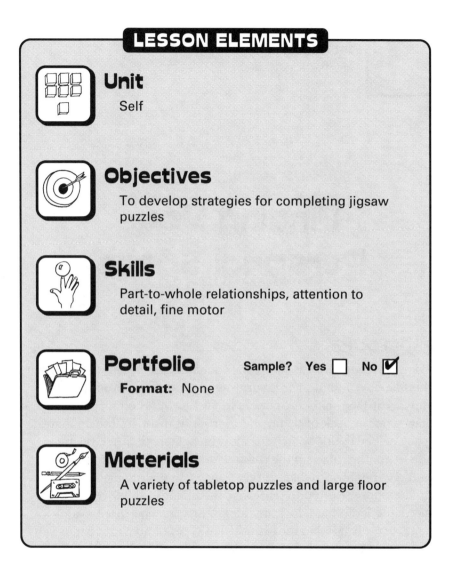

LESSON ELEMENTS

Unit
Self

Objectives
To develop strategies for completing jigsaw puzzles

Skills
Part-to-whole relationships, attention to detail, fine motor

Portfolio
Sample? Yes ☐ No ☑
Format: None

Materials
A variety of tabletop puzzles and large floor puzzles

COMMENTS
Children may want to compare puzzles by the number of pieces in each.

Intelligence
Bodily-Kinesthetic

Finding Your Personal Space

PROCEDURE

Ask children to walk around the room and explore the space. When children have found their favorite spot ask them to sit in the space and give it their name. Ask them to notice who is on their left, on their right, in back of them, and in front of them. Tell them that this space will be their "home" for movement activities. Ask them to hop to another place in the room. Use the drum as a signal for children to return to their "home" space. In their home spaces, have children brainstorm different ways their hands can move. Discuss speed and level (high, low, middle) of movements. Discuss additional ways hands can move and what types of activities hands can engage in. Allow time for demonstration by all children. Teach the song "Early in the Morning" which begins "This is the way we. . ." Ask children to volunteer hand and/or body movement ideas for new action verses to the song.

GUIDING QUESTIONS

- What are some ways you can tell that you are in your "home" space?
- Can you think of ways to move your hands to imitate doing something (like peeling a banana, playing a guitar)?

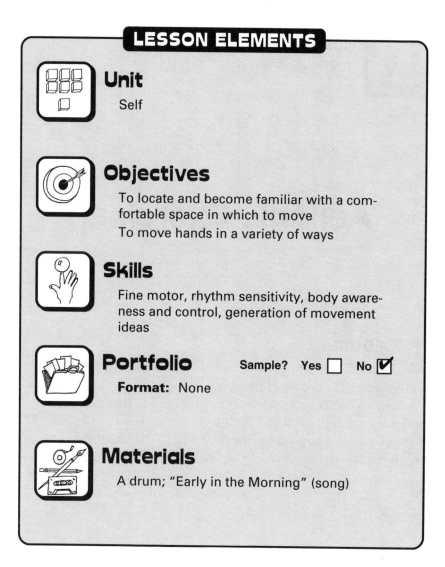

LESSON ELEMENTS

Unit
Self

Objectives
To locate and become familiar with a comfortable space in which to move
To move hands in a variety of ways

Skills
Fine motor, rhythm sensitivity, body awareness and control, generation of movement ideas

Portfolio
Sample? Yes ☐ No ☑
Format: None

Materials
A drum; "Early in the Morning" (song)

COMMENTS

Teachers should feel free to use selections from movement records they have in their classrooms.

Intelligence
Bodily-Kinesthetic

Aerobic Exercise

PROCEDURE

Ask children if they know what "aerobic" exercise is. Discuss how exercise helps the body and the mind. Talk about the importance of warming up and cooling down. Direct children in stretching exercises. Play aerobics selections from record or tape. After cool down, discuss how it felt to have the heart beating, to be breathing hard, and to feel sweaty. Have children play "follow-the-exercise-leader"; ask for volunteers to lead the class in large and/or small movements. Use a kitchen timer to set limits. Allow time for all children who would like to take a turn to lead.

GUIDING QUESTIONS

- What do you suppose a large movement would look like? a small movement?
- What is it like for you to move fast? slow?

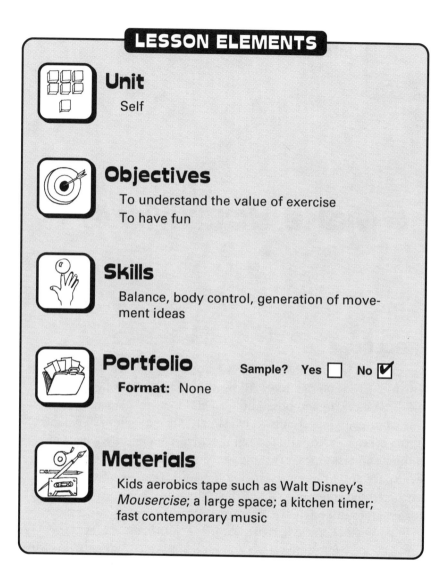

LESSON ELEMENTS

Unit
Self

Objectives
To understand the value of exercise
To have fun

Skills
Balance, body control, generation of movement ideas

Portfolio
Format: None

Sample? Yes ☐ No ☑

Materials
Kids aerobics tape such as Walt Disney's *Mousercise*; a large space; a kitchen timer; fast contemporary music

COMMENTS

Allow children to bring in their favorite music from home for dancing. Play "follow the leader."

Intelligence
Bodily-Kinesthetic

Make your Move

PROCEDURE

Ask children to find their "home" space. Ask children if they know how to balance on one foot. Allow some to demonstrate, pointing out differences in methods. Allow all children to balance on one foot while everyone counts to ten slowly, then all children balance on the other foot counting to ten quickly. Ask children what kinds of things go fast and what things go slow. Ask children to find their own space and to listen to an action record. Discuss how the record instructed the children to move (fast, slow, like a cat, etc.). Brainstorm names of body parts. Choose different ways to move those body parts (shake, wave, twist, etc.). Teach the song "Hey, Hey This-A-Way." Ask children to volunteer movement ideas by describing or demonstrating actions. Incorporate children's movement ideas into new song verses.

GUIDING QUESTIONS

- What parts of your body can you move?
- How can you move the parts of your body?
- How do you feel when you move your body in unfamiliar ways?

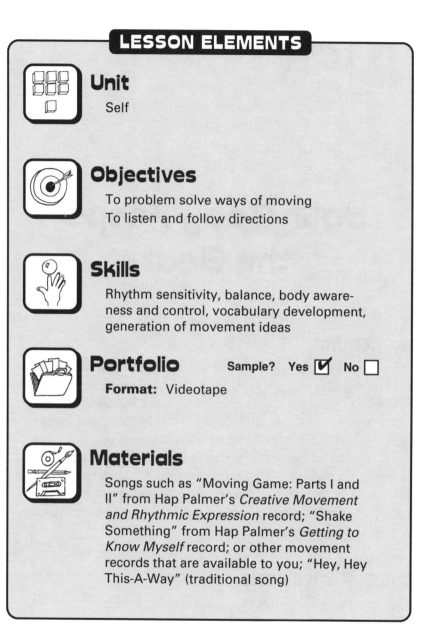

LESSON ELEMENTS

Unit
Self

Objectives
To problem solve ways of moving
To listen and follow directions

Skills
Rhythm sensitivity, balance, body awareness and control, vocabulary development,
generation of movement ideas

Portfolio   Sample? Yes ☑ No ☐
Format: Videotape

Materials
Songs such as "Moving Game: Parts I and
II" from Hap Palmer's *Creative Movement
and Rhythmic Expression* record; "Shake
Something" from Hap Palmer's *Getting to
Know Myself* record; or other movement
records that are available to you; "Hey, Hey
This-A-Way" (traditional song)

COMMENTS
Ask children if they know any other songs to sing. Let children
generate ideas for creating movements to go with their suggestions.
Videotape children moving to songs.

Intelligence
Musical

Your Body Keeps the Beat

PROCEDURE

Tap a beat in a variey of ways using feet, hands, or lap (patschen) by snapping, clapping, slapping, etc. Children should imitate. Have children find their own space. Sing "Head and Shoulders" varying tempo (speed) and dynamic (volume) as children sing and move to the song. Unfamiliar verses may be added for surprise.

Have paired children find a way to keep the beat to accompany the rhyme: "I do love _____ on my pizza-o." On each repetition ask children to find a new way to keep the beat and invent a new topping for the pizza-o. End by keeping the beat to a familiar song of the children's choice.

GUIDING QUESTIONS

- What parts of your body can you use to keep the beat?
- What ideas for keeping the beat did you share with your partner?

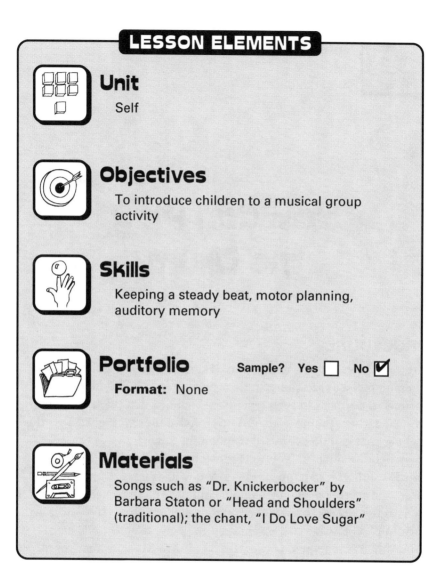

LESSON ELEMENTS

Unit
Self

Objectives
To introduce children to a musical group activity

Skills
Keeping a steady beat, motor planning, auditory memory

Portfolio
Format: None

Sample? Yes ☐ No ☑

Materials
Songs such as "Dr. Knickerbocker" by Barbara Staton or "Head and Shoulders" (traditional); the chant, "I Do Love Sugar"

COMMENTS

Let children volunteer to share their favorite way to keep the beat and to explain why.

Intelligence
Musical

You Can Play the Drum

PROCEDURE

Keep the beat, varying tempo and dynamics. Have children imitate and add facial expressions. In their own space, let children perform actions to a song. On each repetition, change pitch (high, medium, low) and affect (happy, sad, grumpy). Ask children to generate other feelings that can be expressed through the rhyme.

Teach the song "If You're Happy and You Know It." Change words to "If you're happy and you know it—play a drum." Demonstrate the correct playing technique and passing sequence. Distribute four or five drums. Repeat the song until all children have had a turn to play. Repeat, asking children to generate additional emotions other than happy. Close with "You Are My Sunshine" or a favorite song.

GUIDING QUESTIONS

- How do you feel sometimes?
- How could you sing or speak to show that feeling?
- How would you play the drum differently to sound happy, sad, tired, etc.?

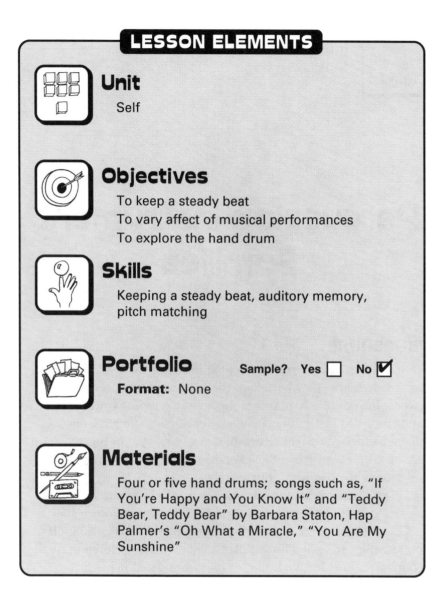

LESSON ELEMENTS

Unit
Self

Objectives
To keep a steady beat
To vary affect of musical performances
To explore the hand drum

Skills
Keeping a steady beat, auditory memory,
pitch matching

Portfolio
Format: None

Sample? Yes ☐ No ☑

Materials
Four or five hand drums; songs such as, "If
You're Happy and You Know It" and "Teddy
Bear, Teddy Bear" by Barbara Staton, Hap
Palmer's "Oh What a Miracle," "You Are My
Sunshine"

COMMENTS

Place charts with familiar chants in the music center and let children
invent ways to keep a steady beat with their body and/or a hand
drum while "reading" the charts.

Intelligence
Musical

Percussion Instrument Families

PROCEDURE

Have children imitate you by keeping the beat. Use a lot of variety. Ask children how they have kept the rhythm during previous lessons. Introduce instrument families as instrument voices that sound alike. Match sounds to action: click (snap fingers), jingle (shake hands), rattle (shake head), scrape (slide palms together), ring (pat head). Teach rhyme: "Click, jingle, rattle, scrape, ring—What will it do when you want it to sing?"

Let children predict what sound (click, jingle, rattle, scrape, or ring) each instrument will make and then test predictions.

Group instruments together by the sound they make. Sing "If you're happy and you know it play a click" while children in small groups with instruments listen for their sound and play.

GUIDING QUESTIONS

- Is there a way you could make another sound with this instrument?
- What was your favorite sound? Why?

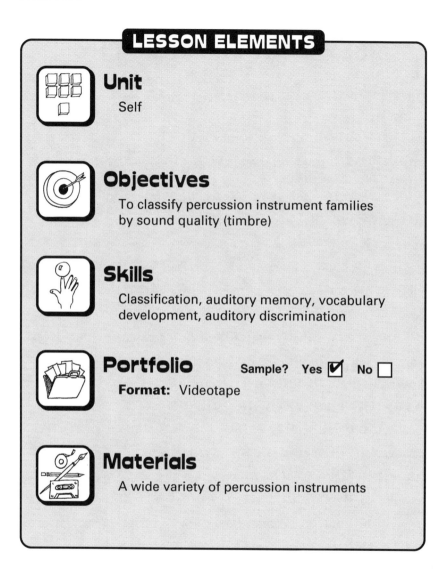

LESSON ELEMENTS

Unit
Self

Objectives
To classify percussion instrument families by sound quality (timbre)

Skills
Classification, auditory memory, vocabulary development, auditory discrimination

Portfolio
Sample? Yes ☑ No ☐

Format: Videotape

Materials
A wide variety of percussion instruments

COMMENTS

Children will discover that instruments are capable of more than one sound but are best at one or two. Let children decide which group these instruments belong with.

SELF UNIT BIBLIOGRAPHY

Aardema, V. (1988). *The Vingananee and the Tree Toad*. New York: Puffin Books.

Aliki. (1984). *Feelings*. New York: Greenwillow Press.

Barrett, J. (1988). *Animals Should Definitely Not Wear Clothing*. New York: MacMillan Child Group.

Barrett, J. (1981). *I'm Too Small, You're Too Big*. New York: Atheneum.

Bridwell, N. (1984). *Clifford's Family*. New York: Scholastic.

Brown, M. W. (1949). *The Important Book*. New York: HarperCollins.

Graham, A. (1987). *Who Wants Arthur?* Milwaukee, Wisc.: Gareth Stevens.

Hoban, R. (1964). *A Baby Sister for Frances*. New York: HarperCollins.

Hoban, R. (1960). *Bedtime for Frances*. New York: HarperCollins.

Hoberman, M. A. (1982). *A House is a House for Me*. New York: Puffin Books.

Hutchins, P. (1986). *The Doorbell Rang*. New York: Greenwillow Press.

Hutchins, P. (1971). *Titch*. New York: Macmillan Child Group, N.Y.

Jeschke, S. (1981). *Perfect the Pig*. New York: H. Holt & Co.

Johnson, C. (1958). *Harold and the Purple Crayon*. New York: HarperCollins.

Johnston, T. (1992). *The Quilt Story*. New York: Putnam.

Keats, E. J. (1972). *Pet Show*. New York: Macmillan Child Group.

Kraus, Robert. (1970). *Whose Mouse Are You?* New York: Macmillan.

Krauss, Ruth. (1953). *A Very Special House*. New York: HarperCollins.

LeSieg, T. (1972). *In a People House*. New York: Random Books.

Lionni, L. (1973). *Swimmy*. New York: Knopf Books.

Marshall, J. (1989). *The True Story of the Three Little Pigs*. New York: Scholastic.

Mayer, M. (1993). *I Was So Mad*. Racine, Wisc.: Western Publishing.

Mayer, M. (1985). *All by Myself*. Racine, Wisc.: Western Publishing.

Mayer, M. (1985). *Me Too!* Racine, Wisc.: Western Publishing.

Mayer, M. (1978). *Little Monster's Neighborhood*. Racine, Wisc.: Western Publishing.

Mayer, M. (1985). *When I Get Bigger.* Racine, Wisc.: Western Publishing.

Mayer, M. (1983). *Just Grandma and Me.* Racine, Wisc.: Western Publishing.

Martin, B. (1983). *Brown Bear, Brown Bear, What Do You See?* New York: H. Holt & Co.

McKissack, P. (1986). *Flossie and the Fox.* New York: Dial Books.

Murphy, J. (1986). *Five Minutes Peace.* New York: Putnam.

Sendak, M. (1985). *Where the Wild Things Are.* New York: HarperCollins.

Sendak, M. (1962). *Pierre.* New York: HarperCollins.

Simon, N. (1974). *Boy Was I Mad!* Chicago: Albert Whitman.

Staton, B., et al. (1988). *Music and You.* New York: MacMillan. (Includes the songs "Dr. Knickerbocker," "Teddy Bear, Teddy Bear," "If You're Happy and You Know It.")

Yashima, T. (1955). *Crow Boy.* New York: Viking Child Books.

Zolotow, C. (1990). *I Like to Be Little.* New York: HarperCollins.

Zolotow, C. (1990). *The Three Billy Goats Gruff, A Norwegian Folktale.* Illustrated by Ellen Appleby. New York: Scholastic.

The *Mousercise* audiotape is available from Walt Disney Productions, Buena Vista Distributors Company, Inc., Burbank, CA 91521.

Creative Movement and Rhythmic Expression and *Getting to Know Myself* records by Hap Palmer are available from Activity Records, Educational Activities, Inc., P.O. Box 392, Freeport, NY 11520.

"Head and Shoulders" Traditional Game Song. *Do It My Way: The Child's Way of Learning,* by Grace C. Nash, Geraldine W. Jones, Barbara A. Potter, Patsy S. Smith. Alfred Publishing Co., Inc. © 1977.

"What a Miracle," words and music by Hap Palmer, published by HAP-PAL Music, Box 323, Topanga, CA 90240. Activity Records, Inc., distributed by Education Activities, Inc., Freeport NY 11520 © 1982.

"You Are My Sunshine," words and music by Jimmie Davis and Charles Mitchell © 1940 (renewed) by Peter International Corp. All Rights Reserved. *World of Music* Book 7 by Carmen E Culp, Lawrence Eisman and Mary E. Hoffman, published by Silver, Burdett & Ginn, Inc., Morristown, N.J. © 1990.

Notes

Fall

The following unit, Fall, focuses on the changes that take place in the child's environment.

OBJECTIVES

- To develop an awareness of seasonal changes

- To understand how seasonal changes affect the lives of people and animals

FALL UNIT OUTLINE

 LINGUISTIC

Fall Mystery Box   Children listen to the teacher describe a hidden object and ask questions to reveal additional clues.

Fall Scavenger Hunt   Children follow teacher's directions to locate hidden fall objects.

Fall Riddles   Autumn objects are described through riddles and children create their own riddles.

 **LOGICAL-MATHEMATICAL**

Pumpkin Estimation   Children play twenty questions. After uncovering a pumpkin, they cut string to estimate its circumference and guess its weight.

Fall Furniture Measurement   Children use a variety of objects including seed pods, Unifix™ cubes, uniform sized leaves, paper clips, colored links, etc., to explore linear measurement using classroom furniture.

Autumn Waves   Children explore three water stations. At one station children experiment with objects that sink or float, at another children make "leaf" boats and race them, and at the third, children engage in free exploration with tubes, pumps, funnels, etc.

SPATIAL/ARTISTIC

Autumn Leaves Mural   Children tear colored paper and glue pieces on large craft paper to create fall forest scenes.

Leaf Rubbings   Children collect fall leaves and explore their designs and patterns through rubbings.

Leaf People   Children use collected leaves, paper scraps, and crayon shavings to create leaf people between sheets of waxed paper.

INTER- AND INTRAPERSONAL/SOCIAL

Pass the Acorns   Children play a cooperative game with acorns.

Moving On   Children relate fears and experiences of families relocating to fall animal migration.

Animal Houses   After discussing how animals collect food and prepare their homes in the fall, children use boxes, tunnels, and blankets to role play animals cooperating in their habitats.

 SPATIAL/ASSEMBLY

Pine Cone Creatures   Children use pine cones, wire, pipe cleaners, and materials found in nature to create people and animals.

Create a Tree   Children construct tree models with clay and objects found in nature.

How Objects Fall, Roll, and Slide   After discussing multiple meanings for the word "fall," children construct a ramp using common objects, predict how objects will move, and record their findings.

 BODILY-KINESTHETIC

Blankets Keep You Warm   After discussing seasonal temperature changes, small groups of children discover how they can use and play with blankets. Each group shares and demonstrates its favorite technique.

Falling Leaves   Children move their bodies like leaves, floating, twisting, drifting, etc. to different types of music.

Squirrels in Trees   In an outdoor game children "collect" nuts and scamper to the "trees" to avoid predators.

 MUSICAL

Sounds of Fall I   After discussing the sounds of fall and how they are different from summer sounds, children explore the percussion family of instruments including claves, sticks, bells, triangles, shakers, etc.

Sounds of Fall II   Children continue their exploration of percussion instruments with special focus on fast/slow, high/low, and soft/loud sounds.

Long and Short   After discussing the long nights and short days of fall, children sort (categorize) percussion instruments by long and short sounds and make patterns using the instruments.

VOCABULARY

This vocabulary list includes language that is used in the lessons for this unit. At the beginning of a lesson you can introduce key words and ask the children to define them and present materials for labeling. Language that you have introduced and that children have generated is used throughout a lesson. After a lesson let children re-evaluate their definitions and clarify meaning for themselves.

acorn	mystery
apple	names of migrating
autumn	animals
branch	orchard
burrow	pine cone
carve	position words
cave	(behind, between,etc.)
changing	pumpkin
chestnut	raking
den	riddle
estimate	roll
fall	scamper
faster	scavenger hunt
float	scurry
forest animal	seed pods
freeze	shorter
glide	sink
gourd	slide
habitats	slower
hay	squash
Indian corn	tree trunk
inspector	twig
instrument names	
(maracas, rhythm	
sticks, etc.)	
leaf	
leaves	
longer	
measure	
migrating	

Unit: Fall
Lesson Plans

Intelligence
Linguistic

Fall Mystery Box

PROCEDURE

All objects are placed out of sight in a "mystery box." The teacher describes one object. For example, "It is hard, brown, and smooth. I can hold it in one hand. You might find it on the ground under a tree." Explain to the children that they must ask questions to guess the identity of the object. (Let children give examples of how to ask questions as language models for peers. For example, "Is it a chestnut?") As children become more familiar with the game, provide them with fewer clues and encourage them to ask more questions to uncover information or to guess the name of the object.

GUIDING QUESTIONS

- What did you hear that made you think of the object you named?
- If you want to know more about the object, what question can you ask?

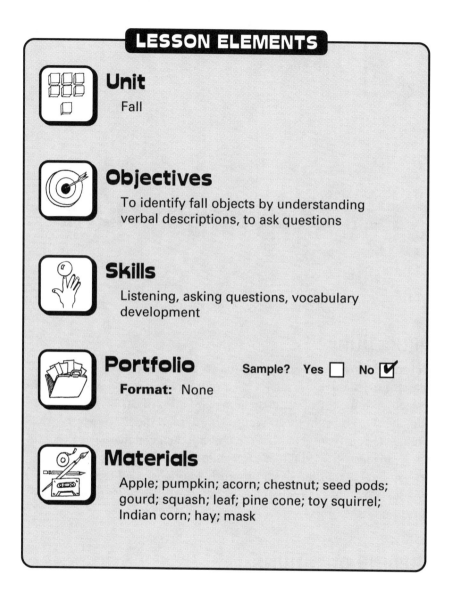

LESSON ELEMENTS

Unit
Fall

Objectives
To identify fall objects by understanding verbal descriptions, to ask questions

Skills
Listening, asking questions, vocabulary development

Portfolio
Format: None

Sample? Yes ☐ No ☑

Materials
Apple; pumpkin; acorn; chestnut; seed pods; gourd; squash; leaf; pine cone; toy squirrel; Indian corn; hay; mask

COMMENTS

Prior to this lesson have children bring in objects to add to a fall scene. Choose objects for the mystery box from this display. Let children use the mystery box during free exploration in the language center.

Intelligence
Linguistic

Fall Scavenger Hunt

PROCEDURE

Before children arrive, hide fall objects out of sight around the classroom. Make a list for yourself of all locations where objects are placed, and for the class, make a list and a set of cards naming all the objects. To begin the scavenger hunt, read the list of objects that are mysteriously missing. Let the children be detectives by calling each "Inspector _____." Let each child choose a card at random from a bag, match the word or words to the list, and tape the card beside its match. Let each child follow a set of oral directions to the location of the object.

GUIDING QUESTIONS

- How will you be able to match the words?
- How do you think you could find a hidden object?
- How did you know where to find the object?
- What directions gave you the most help?

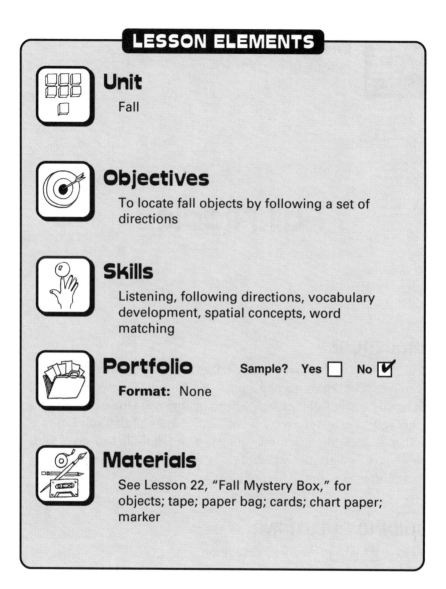

LESSON ELEMENTS

Unit

Fall

Objectives

To locate fall objects by following a set of directions

Skills

Listening, following directions, vocabulary development, spatial concepts, word matching

Portfolio   Sample?   Yes ☐   No ☑

Format: None

Materials

See Lesson 22, "Fall Mystery Box," for objects; tape; paper bag; cards; chart paper; marker

COMMENTS

In your description include references to position (left, right, beside, behind, between, in front, forward, backward, up, down, on, off, in, out, under), colors, and shapes.

Intelligence
Linguistic

Fall Riddles

PROCEDURE

Begin by asking children to solve fall riddles (see page 66). For example, "I am thinking of a round, red fruit that grows in an orchard. I might say 'I crunch when you bite me. One of me a day helps keep the doctor away. What am I?'" Let children solve the riddles. Ask children to think up their own fall riddles to share with the class. Children may work in pairs and may need objects or photographs for stimulation of ideas.

GUIDING QUESTIONS

- How did you know I was describing _____?
- What do you think were the most important clues in your riddle?
- How did you make up that riddle?
- What were you thinking that helped you make up the riddle?

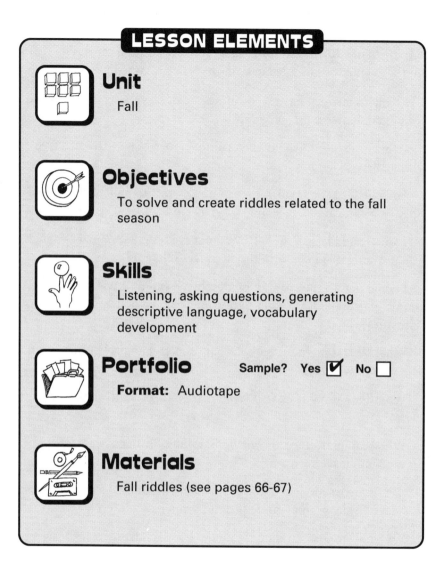

LESSON ELEMENTS

Unit
Fall

Objectives
To solve and create riddles related to the fall season

Skills
Listening, asking questions, generating descriptive language, vocabulary development

Portfolio
Sample? Yes ☑ No ☐
Format: Audiotape

Materials
Fall riddles (see pages 66-67)

COMMENTS
This lesson could be used during any unit to reinforce vocabulary and creative expression through language.

HOMEWORK
Children make up riddles on any subject at home and share them with the class.

FALL RIDDLES

I am the name of a season. My days are shorter than my nights. I am another name for fall. I begin with the letter A. What's my name?

I hang in a tree. I have seeds in me. I can be yellow, green, or red. I am juicy. I am a fruit. What am I?

I die in the fall. I usually turn colors before I die. I am on a tree with acorns. What am I?

I can be large or small. You can make me into a pie. I grow on a vine. You can carve a face in me. What am I?

I am around less in the fall. Without me, you have a hard time seeing. I shine the longest in the summer. What am I?

I come out on the last day in October. I can be a witch, cat, bunny, ghost, and lots more. I go from house to house. I like candy. Who am I?

What flies at night, eats insects, and sleeps hanging upside down in caves all winter?

What flies at night, is said to be wise, and asks the question, "Who?"

Who scampers along the ground looking for nuts, is gray or brown, and has a bushy tail?

Who scurries along stone walls, has brown and white stripes on its side, and sleeps in an underground tunnel all winter?

Who has no arms and no legs but slithers underground to sleep for the winter?

Who joins its friends in the sky forming the letter V as they honk and fly south to a warmer place to spend the winter?

Who is big, furry, eats honey, and sleeps in a den?

Who has gray feathers and a red breast and leaves its nest to fly south for the winter?

Who has wings, sips nectar from flowers, lives in a hive, and makes honey?

What fruit keeps you healthy, cleans your teeth, grows on a tree, and goes "munch, crunch, crunch" when you eat it?

What can be red, small, hard, and sour, but can also be green, plump, juicy, and sweet?

What has a trunk, bark, limbs, and seeds called acorns?

Intelligence
Logical-Mathematical

Pumpkin Estimation

PROCEDURE

With a pumpkin concealed in the box, play the attributes game of twenty questions. Model questions for children to ask. Review information that they have learned through questioning. Keep a record of "yes" responses on the chalkboard. As questions are asked, children keep a tally to twenty. Review all "yes" answers and give every child an opportunity to guess what's in the box. After taking the pumpkin out of the box, have each child cut a piece of string that they think is long enough to wrap around the circumference of the pumpkin. Have each child use his or her string to measure the pumpkin, and then attach the string to the graph.

GUIDING QUESTIONS

- What objects can you think of that might fit in this box?
- What objects do you know would not fit in the box?
- How do you suppose you could find out what's in the box?
- How will you decide where to cut the string?

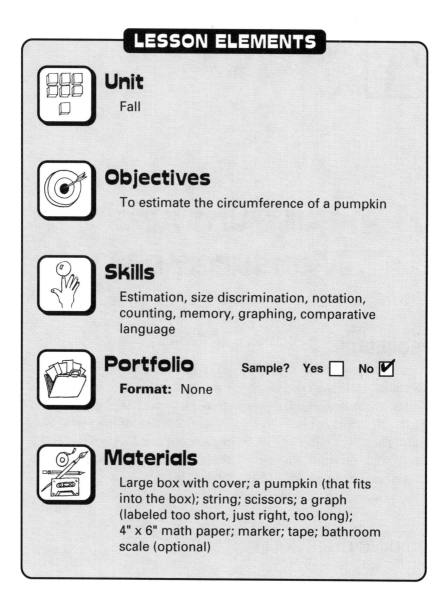

LESSON ELEMENTS

Unit
Fall

Objectives
To estimate the circumference of a pumpkin

Skills
Estimation, size discrimination, notation, counting, memory, graphing, comparative language

Portfolio
Format: None

Sample?   Yes ☐   No ☑

Materials
Large box with cover; a pumpkin (that fits into the box); string; scissors; a graph (labeled too short, just right, too long); 4" x 6" math paper; marker; tape; bathroom scale (optional)

COMMENTS

Children can estimate the weight of the pumpkin (need bathroom scale). Children can graph the kind of face they want to carve into the pumpkin.

Intelligence
Logical-Mathematical

Fall Furniture Measurement

PROCEDURE

Have children choose a unit of measurement (e.g., Unifix™ cubes, seed pods, or leaves) and an object to measure (e.g., desk). Let them predict how many units of measurement they will need to measure the length, width, or height of the object, and record their predictions. Then ask children to measure the object and record the results. (For example, an easel might be six seed pods wide.) After the measurements are recorded, pairs of children can share their results comparing their predictions with the actual measurements.

GUIDING QUESTIONS

- How did you decide on _____ as your prediction?
- What happened when you measured the _____ with your Unifix cubes?
- Were you surprised by the actual measurements?

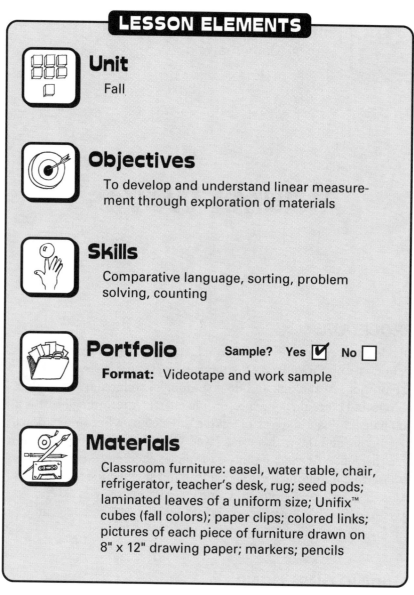

LESSON ELEMENTS

Unit
Fall

Objectives
To develop and understand linear measurement through exploration of materials

Skills
Comparative language, sorting, problem solving, counting

Portfolio
Sample? Yes ☑ No ☐

Format: Videotape and work sample

Materials
Classroom furniture: easel, water table, chair, refrigerator, teacher's desk, rug; seed pods; laminated leaves of a uniform size; Unifix™ cubes (fall colors); paper clips; colored links; pictures of each piece of furniture drawn on 8" x 12" drawing paper; markers; pencils

COMMENTS

To make this lesson easier for younger children, pair the children and give them a piece of paper with a picture or drawing of the object they are measuring. Have a column for predictions and a column for actual measurement count.

71

Intelligence
Logical-Mathematical

Autumn Waves

PROCEDURE

Divide children into small groups. Have three different water
stations set up for sink and float experiences, boat races, and free
exploration. At the sink and float station, let children freely explore
objects and place them on a recording chart. (A recording chart is a
laminated 12" x 18" piece of oaktag, divided by a line drawn down
the middle, and the words "sink" and "float" and a picture drawn
on either side.) At the boat race station, let children construct boats
by inserting a toothpick through a leaf and sticking the toothpick
through a piece of styrofoam. Using straws, children can explore
ways to make their boats move. At the water table, children can
explore conservation properties.

GUIDING QUESTIONS

- Which of these objects do you think will float? sink? Why?
- Which objects surprised you? Why?
- How did you get your boat to move?
- How could you make your boat move faster?

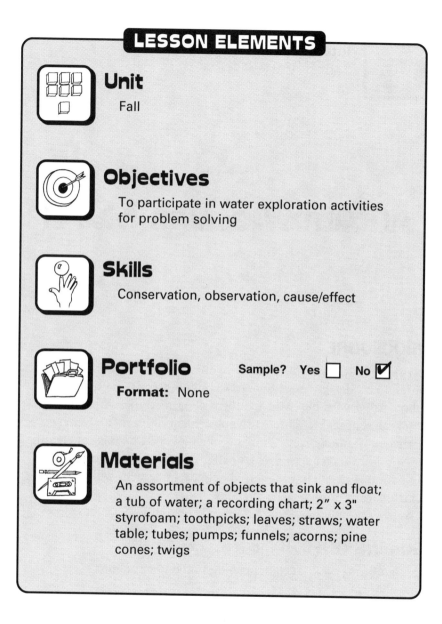

LESSON ELEMENTS

Unit
Fall

Objectives
To participate in water exploration activities for problem solving

Skills
Conservation, observation, cause/effect

Portfolio
Sample? Yes ☐ No ☑
Format: None

Materials
An assortment of objects that sink and float; a tub of water; a recording chart; 2" x 3" styrofoam; toothpicks; leaves; straws; water table; tubes; pumps; funnels; acorns; pine cones; twigs

COMMENTS

This lesson could be done in two thirty-minute sessions or longer in order to afford each child ample exploration time.

Intelligence
Spatial/Artistic

Autumn Leaves Mural

PROCEDURE

Let children tell what they know about autumn. After a discussion of fall trees, display materials. Ask children to imagine filling the whole paper with big trees. Let them describe the size needed for trunks and branches. Discuss the placement of leaves attached to branches, of falling leaves, and of fallen leaves. Demonstrate tearing strips and round shapes. Let a small group of children be responsible for one tree. They may need help deciding who will work on which part or how to share the jobs.

GUIDING QUESTIONS

- What have you noticed happening to the trees in your neighborhood?
- How could you use this colored paper to create pictures of autumn trees?
- How did you decide who would work on which part of the tree in your small group?

74

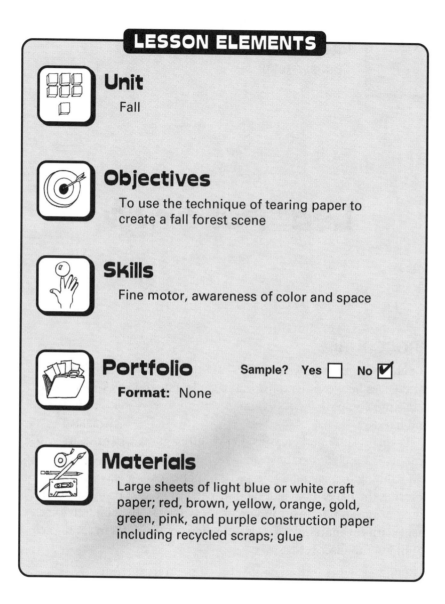

LESSON ELEMENTS

Unit
Fall

Objectives
To use the technique of tearing paper to create a fall forest scene

Skills
Fine motor, awareness of color and space

Portfolio
Sample? Yes ☐ No ☑

Format: None

Materials
Large sheets of light blue or white craft paper; red, brown, yellow, orange, gold, green, pink, and purple construction paper including recycled scraps; glue

COMMENTS

At another time, children may want to make additions to this scene, such as migrating birds or people raking.

Intelligence
Spatial/Artistic

Leaf Rubbings

PROCEDURE

Let children examine leaves and share their observations. Discuss differences between the topside and underside of leaves. Discuss leaf veins and compare them to human veins. Observe veins in wrists and hands.

Display paper and crayons. Let children guess what the art lesson will be. Let a child demonstrate a leaf rubbing. (A child can make a leaf rubbing by placing a thin piece of paper over a leaf and evenly coloring the paper with a crayon or pencil.) Predict problems that could occur and brainstorm ways to solve them. Let children experiment with the materials. To close the lesson, let children share their rubbings and discoveries.

GUIDING QUESTIONS

- What do you notice when you look carefully at a leaf?
- What job do you think the veins do for the leaf?
- Which of your rubbings do you like best? Why?
- How did you make it?

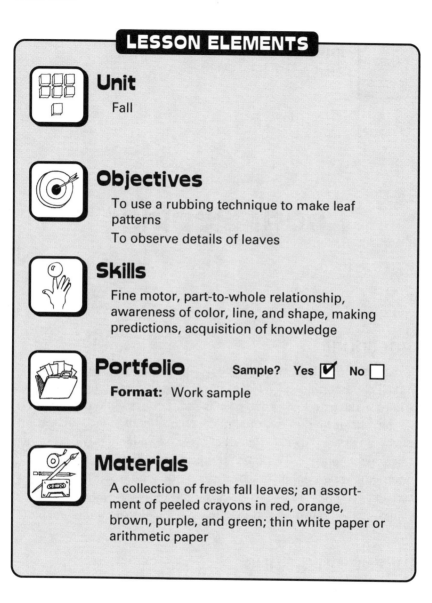

LESSON ELEMENTS

Unit
Fall

Objectives
To use a rubbing technique to make leaf patterns
To observe details of leaves

Skills
Fine motor, part-to-whole relationship, awareness of color, line, and shape, making predictions, acquisition of knowledge

Portfolio   Sample? Yes ☑ No ☐
Format: Work sample

Materials
A collection of fresh fall leaves; an assortment of peeled crayons in red, orange, brown, purple, and green; thin white paper or arithmetic paper

COMMENTS
You may choose to assign homework after this lesson.

HOMEWORK
Make rubbings of objects at home.

Intelligence
Spatial/Artistic

Leaf People

PROCEDURE

Display materials and ask children what they think the activity will be. Tell children that since leaves have veins we are going to use them to make people who have veins too. Let one child choose a leaf that she or he thinks would make a good body. Place the leaf on a sheet of waxed paper. Let another child add a leaf body part of his or her own choosing. Continue taking turns adding leaf body parts until the figure is complete. Cover the figure with a second sheet of waxed paper and iron between several pieces of newspaper. Let children make their own leaf people.

GUIDING QUESTIONS

- When making a person, what parts of the body do you think are the most important?
- How could you use these materials to look like body parts?
- How would you use an acorn?
- What body part could crayon shavings be?

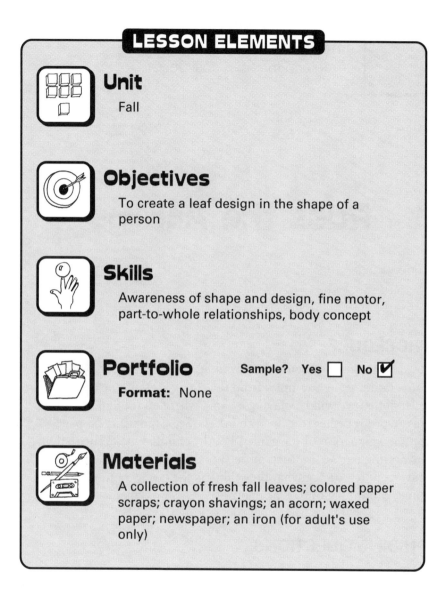

LESSON ELEMENTS

Unit
Fall

Objectives
To create a leaf design in the shape of a person

Skills
Awareness of shape and design, fine motor, part-to-whole relationships, body concept

Portfolio
Sample? Yes ☐ No ☑

Format: None

Materials
A collection of fresh fall leaves; colored paper scraps; crayon shavings; an acorn; waxed paper; newspaper; an iron (for adult's use only)

COMMENTS

Children may want to make leaf animals too.

Intelligence
Inter- and Intrapersonal/Social

Pass the Acorns

PROCEDURE

Read the folktale. Discuss the advantages and disadvantages of cooperation using examples from the story. Present one acorn and tell children we will be playing a game where all the children in the class work together to help each other. (See Comments on page 81 for an explanation of the game.) Let the children make suggestions for passing one acorn, then more. Try their ideas out in the group. Have children decide what they think is the best way to play the game, continuing to pass as many acorns as possible.

GUIDING QUESTIONS

- How can everybody have a chance to hold the acorn while he remains seated in a circle like we are now?
- How do you suppose we could pass more than one acorn with each person holding only one at a time?
- What do you think is the most number of acorns we could pass and why?
- What are some strategies that you use to make this game work well?

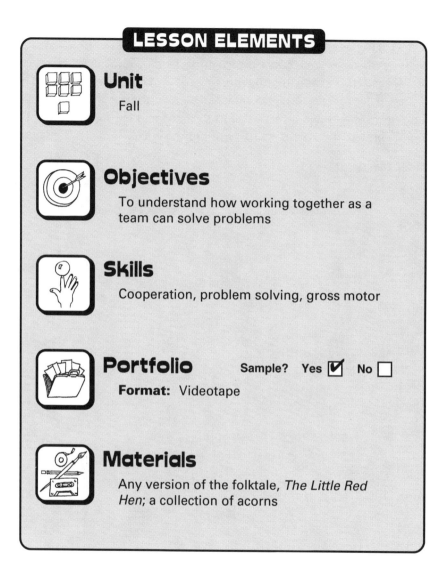

LESSON ELEMENTS

Unit
Fall

Objectives
To understand how working together as a team can solve problems

Skills
Cooperation, problem solving, gross motor

Portfolio
Sample? Yes ☑ No ☐
Format: Videotape

Materials
Any version of the folktale, *The Little Red Hen*; a collection of acorns

COMMENTS

Explanation of game: The object of the game is to cooperate by passing as many acorns as possible around the circle. Each child can hold only one acorn at a time. (The ultimate goal is to pass as many acorns as there are people playing the game.) Begin by practicing with only one acorn. Pass the acorn to the child to your left. That child passes the acorn to the child on his or her left, etc. When the acorn returns to you, the practice ends. Now tell the children that more than one acorn will be passed in the same way as the practice turn. Begin passing a few acorns, one at a time, until the first acorn passed returns to you. Conceal the acorns as they return. When the last acorn returns, ask the students to guess how many acorns were passed. Then let the children count the acorns. Repeat the procedure, increasing the number of acorns passed and letting the children predict how many acorns will go around the circle.

UNIT: FALL

Intelligence
Inter- and Intrapersonal/Social

Moving On

PROCEDURE

Read a story about moving to a new home. Discuss families you know that have moved. Talk about how it feels to leave friends. Discuss reasons for moving including advantages and disadvantages of relocating to a new place. Relate animal migration (e.g., robins, catbirds, Canada geese, Ibis, or humpback whales migrating to climates for survival) to people moving. Discuss how people moving and animal migration are alike and different. Record children's responses on chart paper.

GUIDING QUESTIONS

- How do you suppose it feels to move away and go to live in an unfamiliar place?
- Have you ever moved? If so, how was your new home the same or different from your old home?
- If you were to move, how might your new neighborhood and your old neighborhood be alike? different?

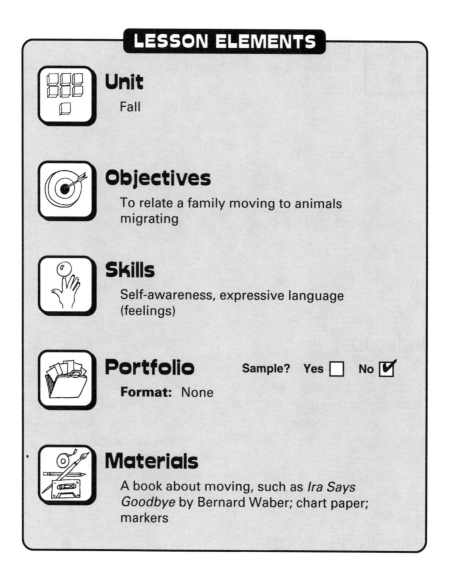

LESSON ELEMENTS

Unit
Fall

Objectives
To relate a family moving to animals migrating

Skills
Self-awareness, expressive language (feelings)

Portfolio
Sample? Yes ☐ No ☑

Format: None

Materials
A book about moving, such as *Ira Says Goodbye* by Bernard Waber; chart paper; markers

COMMENTS
Allow children to bring in photographs of homes where they have lived to share with classmates.

Intelligence
Inter- and Intrapersonal/Social

Animal Houses

PROCEDURE

Using the suggested materials, let children replicate the homes of squirrels, ground hogs, chipmunks, mice, moles, bats, foxes, raccoons, and rabbits (burrows, caves, dens, trees). Discuss how animals use and maintain their homes for rearing their young, for protection, for sleeping, and sometimes for food storage. In small groups, have children imitate and explore animal habitats. After each group has had a turn, discuss the experience, any problems that arose, and how the problems were dealt with or solved.

GUIDING QUESTIONS

- What animal did you pretend to be?
- How did you behave as that animal?
- What do you suppose your animal thinks when he's in his home? outside his home?
- How did you share your small space?
- What did you do to help each other?
- How did each member of your group act toward the other group members?

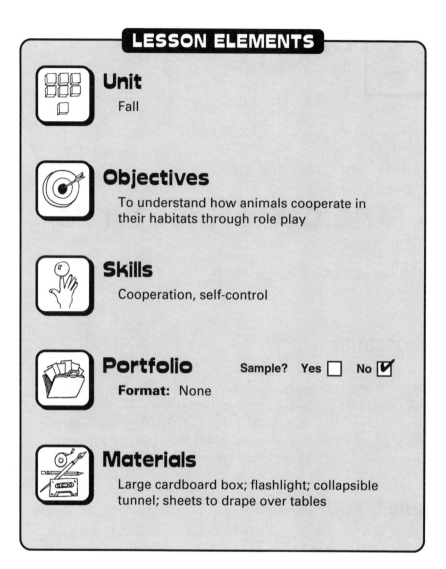

LESSON ELEMENTS

Unit
Fall

Objectives
To understand how animals cooperate in their habitats through role play

Skills
Cooperation, self-control

Portfolio
Sample? Yes ☐ No ☑
Format: None

Materials
Large cardboard box; flashlight; collapsible tunnel; sheets to drape over tables

COMMENTS

Show children pictures of different kinds of houses (e.g., apartments, condos, cottages, etc.) cut from magazines and let them describe how different families live.

Intelligence
Spatial/Assembly

Pine Cone Creatures

PROCEDURE

Display materials and ask children to identify them. Provide children with any unfamiliar vocabulary. Let children decide what kind of creature they will make and have them share their ideas with others. Let children experiment with materials. As closure, share finished creations and discuss successful strategies and problems encountered. Display people and animals in a fall scene.

GUIDING QUESTIONS

- How can you use these materials to make people and animals?
- How can the wire help you?
- What do you think the pipe cleaners could be used for?

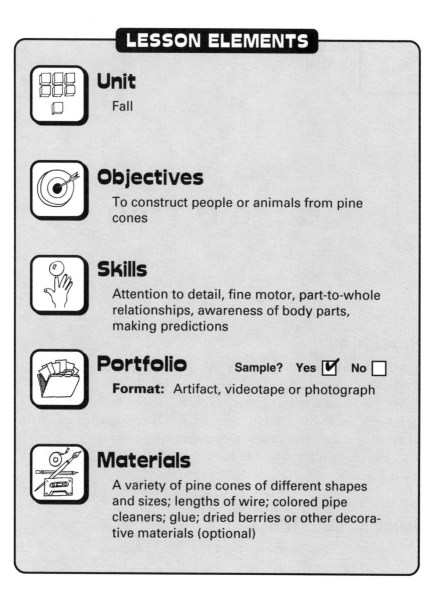

LESSON ELEMENTS

Unit
Fall

Objectives
To construct people or animals from pine cones

Skills
Attention to detail, fine motor, part-to-whole relationships, awareness of body parts, making predictions

Portfolio
Sample? Yes ☑ No ☐

Format: Artifact, videotape or photograph

Materials
A variety of pine cones of different shapes and sizes; lengths of wire; colored pipe cleaners; glue; dried berries or other decorative materials (optional)

COMMENTS
Children may want to add eyes or other decorative features. These materials can be put in the assembly center for further investigation.

Intelligence
Spatial/Assembly

Create a Tree

PROCEDURE

Provide materials and let children tell what they know about them. Introduce any unfamiliar vocabulary. Let a child demonstrate how to roll clay into a tree trunk shape. Let children make suggestions for how to attach branches to the tree trunk. Let children explore materials and construct individual creations. Small pieces of colored tissue or scrap paper may be added as leaves. Trees can be displayed in a fall scene.

GUIDING QUESTIONS

- What have you noticed about the trees we looked at?
- How can these materials be used to make a tree like the ones we've been looking at?
- What color leaves have you observed in these trees?

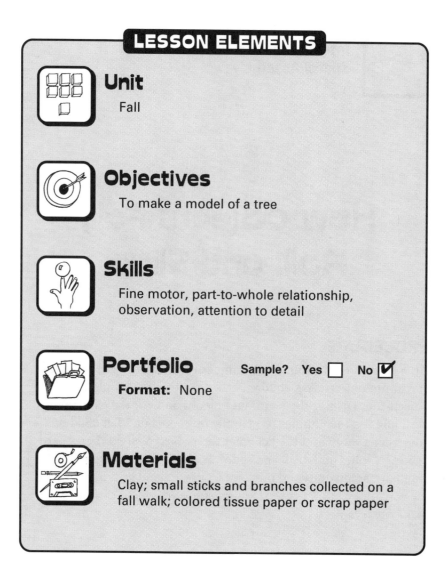

LESSON ELEMENTS

Unit
Fall

Objectives
To make a model of a tree

Skills
Fine motor, part-to-whole relationship, observation, attention to detail

Portfolio
Sample? Yes ☐ No ☑
Format: None

Materials
Clay; small sticks and branches collected on a fall walk; colored tissue paper or scrap paper

COMMENTS

Children should have previously observed, drawn, and discussed a deciduous tree in the school yard or neighborhood. You may want to have reference books about trees available for children to look at.

Intelligence
Spatial/Assembly

How Objects Fall, Roll, and Slide

PROCEDURE

After discussing the multiple meanings of the word "fall," display classroom objects. Ask children how they think we could make the objects fall. Display the board and blocks and ask the children how we could use these things to help the objects "fall." Let children construct a ramp and predict what each object will do. Label cards "slide," "roll," and "roll and slide" as children use these words. Compare predictions and outcomes. Classify and group objects by the way they "fall." Let the children adjust the incline ramp and make observations.

GUIDING QUESTIONS

- What does "fall" mean to you?
- How are you able to guess whether an object will roll or slide?
- How could we make the car roll faster? slower?

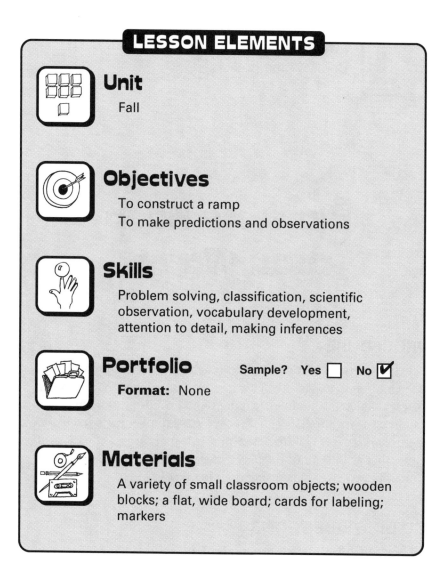

LESSON ELEMENTS

Unit
Fall

Objectives
To construct a ramp
To make predictions and observations

Skills
Problem solving, classification, scientific observation, vocabulary development, attention to detail, making inferences

Portfolio
Sample? Yes ☐ No ☑
Format: None

Materials
A variety of small classroom objects; wooden blocks; a flat, wide board; cards for labeling; markers

COMMENTS
This whole group activity can be explored more thoroughly by children in the assembly center as a follow-up to this lesson.

Intelligence
Bodily-Kinesthetic

Blankets Keep You Warm

PROCEDURE

Let children tell how the weather has changed from summer to fall. Ask children to explain the changes they must make to keep warm. Display blankets and divide children into groups of four. Ask children to work together to discover ways to play with and explore their blankets. Let children have time to experiment. Let each group know that at the end of the play time they will be asked to demonstrate the way they liked using their blanket best.

GUIDING QUESTIONS

- How can you and your group play with this blanket?
- How can you and your group turn this blanket into something new and unusual?
- What other things do we use to keep warm?

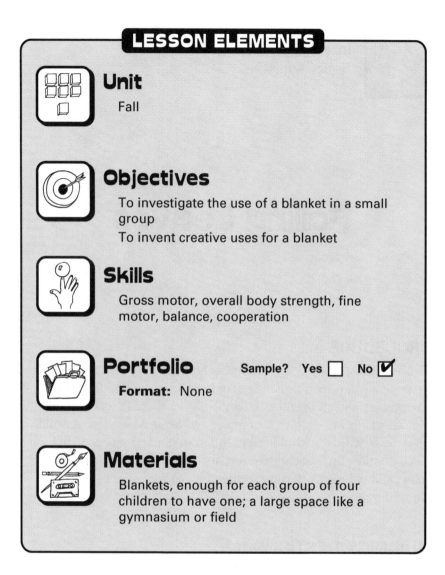

LESSON ELEMENTS

Unit
Fall

Objectives
To investigate the use of a blanket in a small group
To invent creative uses for a blanket

Skills
Gross motor, overall body strength, fine motor, balance, cooperation

Portfolio
Sample? Yes ☐ No ☑
Format: None

Materials
Blankets, enough for each group of four children to have one; a large space like a gymnasium or field

COMMENTS
Watch for the unexpected during free exploration. Let groups explain their choice for demonstration.

Intelligence
Bodily-Kinesthetic

Falling Leaves

PROCEDURE

Generate a list of leaf movement vocabulary such as fly, twist, glide, float, sink, drop, twirl, and bend and qualities, such as fast, slow, smooth, jagged, and gentle. Record children's ideas on chart paper. Play short clips of each type of music and let children describe and/ or show how leaves would fall to different musical pieces. Play each piece of music and let children respond like leaves. As closure let each child tell which music and show which movement she or he enjoyed most.

GUIDING QUESTIONS

- What are some ways you have noticed leaves falling?
- How could you use your body to show the way leaves fall?
- How is drifting different from sliding?
- How could you show with your body the pattern "glide, glide, twirl"?

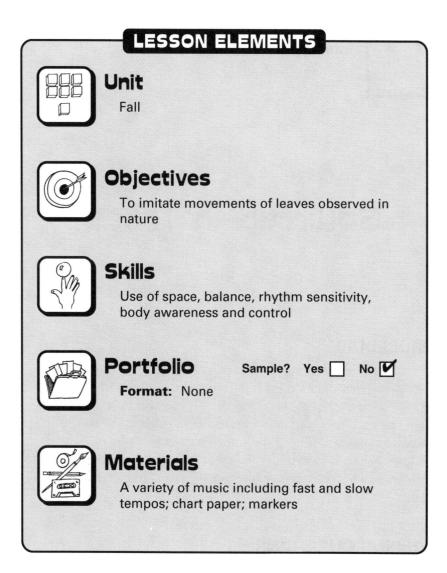

LESSON ELEMENTS

Unit
Fall

Objectives
To imitate movements of leaves observed in nature

Skills
Use of space, balance, rhythm sensitivity, body awareness and control

Portfolio   Sample? Yes ☐   No ☑
Format: None

Materials
A variety of music including fast and slow tempos; chart paper; markers

COMMENTS
"Fall" music such as Scott Joplin's "Maple Leaf Rag," Vivaldi's "The Four Seasons," and Natalie Cole's "Autumn Leaves" is recommended.

Intelligence
Bodily-Kinesthetic

Squirrels in Trees

PROCEDURE

Divide children into groups of three. Have two children join hands to form a "tree" and a third child stand in the middle of the "tree" as the "squirrel." At the sound of the whistle, squirrels should leave their trees and go about their business in the forest. The claves indicate a predator is near and squirrels must hurry home. Let all children have an opportunity to be both stationary trees and squirrels. Let children invent new rules for predators to be included in the game.

GUIDING QUESTIONS

- How can you describe and/or show how squirrels move in their environment?
- How could we change this game to include predators?
- How could we play the game if only two large trees grew in our forest?

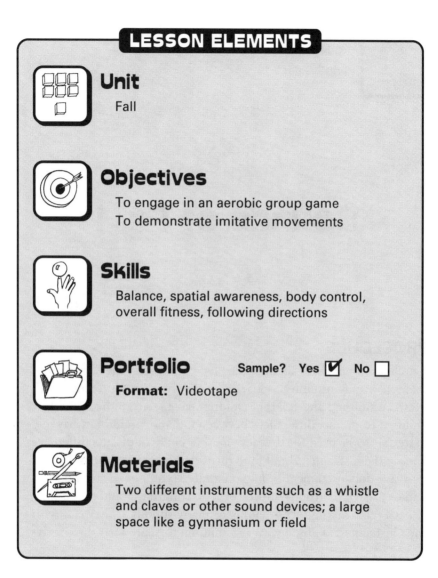

LESSON ELEMENTS

Unit
Fall

Objectives
To engage in an aerobic group game
To demonstrate imitative movements

Skills
Balance, spatial awareness, body control, overall fitness, following directions

Portfolio
Sample? Yes ☑ No ☐
Format: Videotape

Materials
Two different instruments such as a whistle and claves or other sound devices; a large space like a gymnasium or field

COMMENTS
If possible, observe neighborhood squirrels prior to this lesson and generate a list of movement vocabulary such as hop, run, jump, freeze, scamper, and scurry.

Intelligence
Musical

Sounds of Fall I

PROCEDURE

Let children tell what changes they have noticed in their environment now that autumn has arrived. Talk about the differences between summer and fall that children have seen and heard. Ask children to predict differences between fall and winter. Display materials to be used for this activity. Let children discuss differences among the instruments and take turns demonstrating them.

Place one instrument family on a table (you'll need five tables and/or areas). In groups of four or five, children should spend time at each table taking turns making as many sounds as they can with each instrument. Close by asking children to share their discoveries.

GUIDING QUESTIONS

- As fall is different from summer, how are wrist jingles (for example) different from sand blocks?
- How many different sounds can you make with your instrument? Can you demonstrate?
- What sounds can you make that remind you of fall, winter, spring, summer?

100

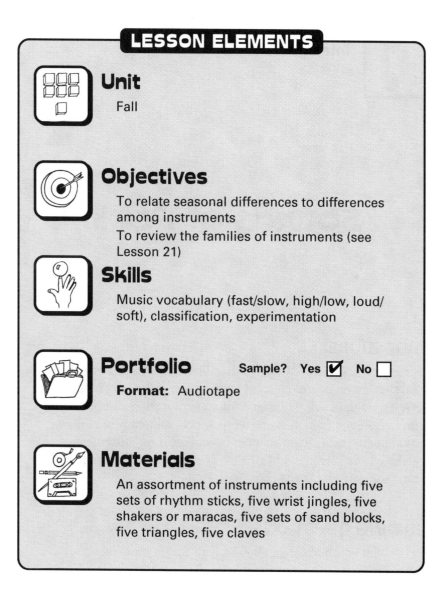

LESSON ELEMENTS

Unit
Fall

Objectives
To relate seasonal differences to differences among instruments

To review the families of instruments (see Lesson 21)

Skills
Music vocabulary (fast/slow, high/low, loud/ soft), classification, experimentation

Portfolio Sample? Yes ☑ No ☐
Format: Audiotape

Materials
An assortment of instruments including five sets of rhythm sticks, five wrist jingles, five shakers or maracas, five sets of sand blocks, five triangles, five claves

COMMENTS
Let children experiment making instrument sounds and recording their music in the music center.

Intelligence
Musical

Sounds of Fall II

PROCEDURE

Using children's ideas about loud and soft fall sounds, have children create repeating sound patterns such as wings flapping (soft) and geese honking (loud). Continue sound exploration and patterning with fast/slow and high/low concepts. Let children take turns making patterns, using instruments, and creating movements as they use the words "long" and "short." To close, let each group demonstrate one pattern for the class.

GUIDING QUESTIONS

- How can you make a soft sound with this instrument? a loud sound?
- How many loud sounds did you use in your pattern? How many soft sounds?
- How would a leaf falling to the ground sound compared to a roaring fire in the fireplace?

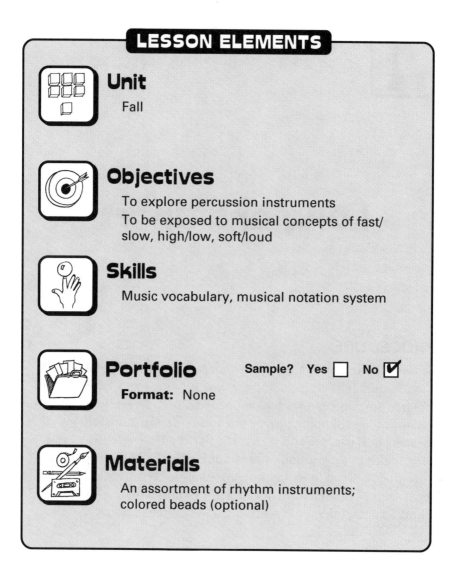

LESSON ELEMENTS

Unit
Fall

Objectives
To explore percussion instruments
To be exposed to musical concepts of fast/
slow, high/low, soft/loud

Skills
Music vocabulary, musical notation system

Portfolio
Sample? Yes ☐ No ☑
Format: None

Materials
An assortment of rhythm instruments;
colored beads (optional)

COMMENTS

Let children use colored beads to make necklace patterns that
represent their loud and soft patterns.

Intelligence
Musical

Long and Short

PROCEDURE

Begin by letting two children play instruments and explain how the sounds are different, including the words "long" and "short." Let children sort instruments by long or short sounds. Let two children play one long-sounding instrument and one short-sounding instrument such as triangle and sticks. Display the Unifix™ cubes. Let a child make a "long sound" (five orange cubes) and a "short sound" (one green) using Unifix cube arrangements. Let another child play the pattern. Let children work in small groups with instruments and Unifix™ cubes, taking turns playing and making patterns.

GUIDING QUESTIONS

- What have you noticed that takes a long time to happen in fall? a short time?
- What instruments make long sounds? short sounds?
- How did you know when to make a long sound? a short sound?

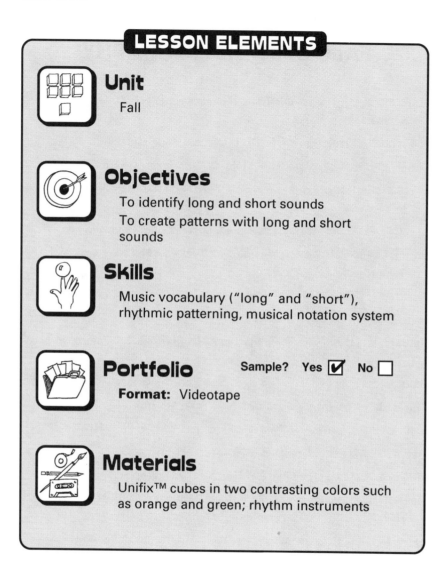

LESSON ELEMENTS

Unit
Fall

Objectives
To identify long and short sounds
To create patterns with long and short sounds

Skills
Music vocabulary ("long" and "short"), rhythmic patterning, musical notation system

Portfolio   Sample?   Yes ☑   No ☐
Format: Videotape

Materials
Unifix™ cubes in two contrasting colors such as orange and green; rhythm instruments

COMMENTS

Let children explore combinations of patterns in the music center. Videotape children making presentations to their peers.

FALL UNIT BIBLIOGRAPHY

Blaire, M. (1975). *The Terrible Thing That Happened at My House*. New York: Scholastic.

Bourgeois, P. (1986). *Franklin In The Dark*. New York: Scholastic.

Curran, E. (1985). *Look at a Tree*. Mohwah, N.J.: Troll Associates.

Eklert, L. (1991). *Red Leaf, Yellow Leaf*. New York: Hartcourt Brace Jovanowich.

Gile, J. (1989). *The First Forest*. Rockford, Ill.: John Gile Communications.

Goss, J. L., and Harste, J. C. (1985). *It Didn't Frighten Me!* St. Petersburg, Fla.: Willowisp Press.

Gruber, S. (1985). *The Monster Under My Bed*. Mahwah, N.J.: Troll Associates.

Hall, D. (1983). *Ox-cart Man*. New York: Puffin Books.

Hubbard, W. (1990). *C is for Curious, an ABC of Feelings*. San Francisco: Chronicle Publishing.

Hutchins, P. (1987). *Changes, Changes*. New York: Macmillan.

Kellogg, S. (1988). *Johnny Appleseed*. New York: Morrow Junior Books.

Kroll, S. (1984). *The Biggest Pumpkin Ever*. New York: Holiday House.

Martin, Bill Jr. (1986). *Barn Dance!* New York: H. Holt & Co.

McQueen, L. (1985). *The Little Red Hen*. New York: Scholastic.

Miller, E. (1971). *Mousekin's Golden House*. Englewood Cliffs, N.J.: Prentice Hall.

Ryder, J. (1989). *Catch the Wind*. New York: Morrow Junior Books.

Scheer, J. (1964). *Rain Makes Applesauce*. New York: Holiday House.

Silverstein, S. (1964). *The Giving Tree*. New York: HarperCollins.

Titherington, J. (1986). *Pumpkin, Pumpkin*. New York: Scholastic.

Waber, B. (1988). *Ira Says Goodbye*. Boston: Houghton Mifflin.

Wildsmith, B. (1992). *Squirrels*. New York: Oxford Press.

Yolen, J. (1987). *Owl Moon*. New York: Putnam.

Day/Night

The following unit, Day/Night, focuses on daily events, dreams and emotions, and celestial observations.

OBJECTIVES

- To develop an awareness and knowledge of celestial changes
- To develop an awareness of daily routines
- To be exposed to the concept of time
- To validate emotions

107

DAY/NIGHT UNIT OUTLINE

 LINGUISTIC

Celestial Poems   After reading a story about the moon, children share observations and create similes for moon poems.

I Can't Sleep   After reading *Ira Sleeps Over* by Bernard Waber, children create a story chart telling what could happen if Ira doesn't get to sleep.

The Best Day   After reading *Alexander and the Terrible, Horrible, No Good, Very Bad Day* by Judith Viorst, children discuss bad things that have happened to them, then they rewrite Viorst's book changing the events of the story to create a wonderful, very best day for Alexander.

 LOGICAL-MATHEMATICAL

Daily Time Line   Children discuss their daily routines and individually sequence their daily activities using original pictures, clothespins, and a clothesline.

Telling Time   After using their homemade clocks, children relate time to their daily activities.

Moon Phases   Children are exposed to the phases of the moon and create their own patterns with moon phase cards.

 SPATIAL/ARTISTIC

Day and Night Contrast Pictures   Children use crayons to depict daytime and nighttime scenes, then cover their drawings with dark or light color washes.

Stained Glass Windows   Children use colored tissue paper, black construction paper, scissors, and glue to create stained glass windows.

The Night Sky   Children create and name their own constellations using Q-tips and white paint on dark paper.

INTER- AND INTRAPERSONAL/SOCIAL

Who's Afraid of the Dark? After listening to a story, children discuss their fears, then experience guided imagery for relaxation.

How Are You Feeling Today? After listening to a story, children identify their feelings and create a class web with yarn.

I'm Not Afraid After listening to *It Didn't Frighten Me* by Janet Goss and Jerome Hurst, children discuss dreams and nightmares and create their own predictable book.

 ## SPATIAL/ASSEMBLY

Paper Clocks Children use paper plates, paper fasteners, markers, and cardboard "hands" to create paper clocks.

Flashlights and Shadows Children explore assembling flashlights and experiment with light and shadow.

Candles Children assemble candle holders using cups, salt, and tall candles.

 ## BODILY-KINESTHETIC

Shadow Tag Children play a chase game where shadows are tagged.

Salute to the Sun Children stretch and strengthen with yoga postures.

Night Moves Guided imagery, dreamy music, and props such as scarves are used to stimulate creative movement.

 ## MUSICAL

Bedtime Song I After listening to a bedtime story, children create their own alphabet song to help them get to sleep.

Bedtime Song II Children choose musical instruments to accompany their "Bedtime Song," then practice and record their song.

Fun with Melodies Children create new songs using old familiar tunes.

VOCABULARY

This vocabulary list includes language that is used in the lessons for this unit. At the beginning of a lesson you can introduce key words and ask the children to define them and present materials for labeling. Language that you have introduced and that children have generated is used throughout a lesson. After a lesson let children re-evaluate their definitions and clarify meaning for themselves.

aerobic	reality
bad	routine
best	second
better	sequence
celestial	smudge
constellations	strategy
crescent moon	tempo
dawn	third
digital clock	twilight
evening	whole
first	worse
fourth	worst
full moon	yoga
galaxy	
good	
half-hour	
hour	
illuminate	
imagination	
last	
lullaby	
melody	
midnight	
Milky Way	
moon phases	
new moon	
noon	
photograph	
posture	
quarter moon	

Unit: Day/Night
Lesson Plans

Intelligence
Linguistic

Celestial Poems

PROCEDURE

After reading a story, ask the children what they have observed about the moon. Record responses on chart paper. Display photographs that include the moon. Record children's comments. Let children respond to the statement "the moon is like _____ because. . . ." Record these statements on crescent moon shapes. Display children's moon poems on a starry night bulletin board along with traditional poems children have learned about the moon and the stars such as "Hey Diddle, Diddle" and "Star Light, Star Bright."

GUIDING QUESTIONS

- What does the moon remind you of?
- What does this photograph of the moon make you think of?
- How do you feel when you look at the full moon? the crescent moon? the new moon?

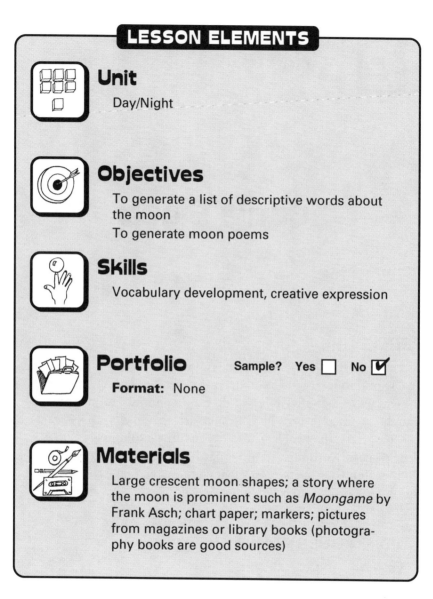

LESSON ELEMENTS

Unit
Day/Night

Objectives
To generate a list of descriptive words about the moon
To generate moon poems

Skills
Vocabulary development, creative expression

Portfolio
Format: None

Sample? Yes ☐ No ☑

Materials
Large crescent moon shapes; a story where the moon is prominent such as *Moongame* by Frank Asch; chart paper; markers; pictures from magazines or library books (photography books are good sources)

COMMENTS

You may choose to assign homework for this lesson.

HOMEWORK

Children may take home a one-month calendar and chart the phases of the moon by making and recording nightly observations.

Intelligence
Linguistic

I Can't Sleep

PROCEDURE

As you read *Ira Sleeps Over*, discuss how Ira's family is helpful or not helpful to him. Stop reading on the next to last page. Change the ending so that after Reggie falls asleep and Ira returns with Tah Tah, he tosses and turns but can't fall asleep. On chart paper record the characters, the problem, and the children's solutions to Ira's sleeplessness. Read the end of Bernard Waber's story. Let the children compare the two different endings and make suggestions for other ways the story could have ended.

GUIDING QUESTIONS

- What helps you get to sleep?
- Why do you suppose Ira's teddy bear isn't helping him?
- What new ways can you think of to help Ira get to sleep?

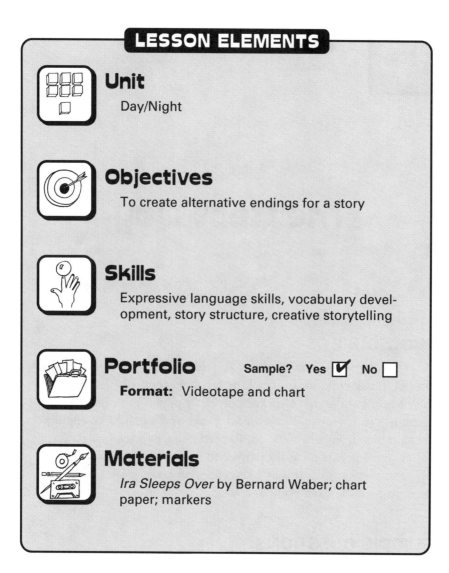

LESSON ELEMENTS

Unit
Day/Night

Objectives
To create alternative endings for a story

Skills
Expressive language skills, vocabulary development, story structure, creative storytelling

Portfolio   Sample?   Yes ☑   No ☐
Format: Videotape and chart

Materials
Ira Sleeps Over by Bernard Waber; chart paper; markers

COMMENTS
You may choose to assign homework after this lesson.

HOMEWORK
Children poll family members asking how each cures sleeplessness.

Intelligence
Linguistic

The Best Day

PROCEDURE

After reading *Alexander and the Terrible, Horrible, No Good, Very Bad Day,* ask children to recall the terrible events of Alexander's day. Record children's responses on chart paper. Arrange their responses in sequence. Review each event and let children change the outcome from bad to good. Record children's responses. Write the changed events on story strips and give one to each child to illustrate. Mount pictures and sentences on larger paper. Sequence these pages to make a book and bind.

GUIDING QUESTIONS

- What kinds of things have happened to you that made you think you were having a bad day? a good day?
- How can you change what happened to Alexander in the shoe store (for example)?

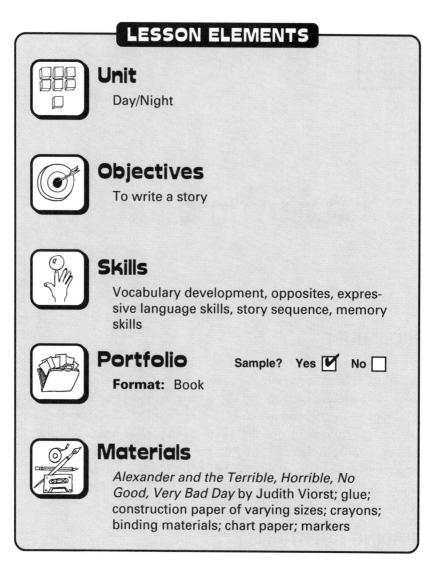

LESSON ELEMENTS

Unit
Day/Night

Objectives
To write a story

Skills
Vocabulary development, opposites, expressive language skills, story sequence, memory skills

Portfolio   Sample? Yes ☑ No ☐
Format: Book

Materials
Alexander and the Terrible, Horrible, No Good, Very Bad Day by Judith Viorst; glue; construction paper of varying sizes; crayons; binding materials; chart paper; markers

COMMENTS
Share the story with another class. Assign homework.

HOMEWORK
Let one child at a time take both the classmade book and Judith Viorst's book home to share with his or her family. Include a journal for parents to record their comments. Each day, read the class the comments from home.

Intelligence
Logical-Mathematical

Daily Time Line

PROCEDURE

In a whole group, each child is given a picture relating to either day or night. Have children put their pictures on either a white or a black clock in sequence according to their daily routine. Give each child a piece of drawing paper. Have children fold the paper into four sections and draw one daily activity in each section. When drawings are complete, let children cut each section to make four pictures. Ask children to put their pictures in sequence and discuss the daily events they have depicted.

GUIDING QUESTIONS

- What kinds of things do you do every day? every night?
- What is the first thing you do in the morning?
- What is something you do in the middle of the day?
- What is the last thing you do at night?

118

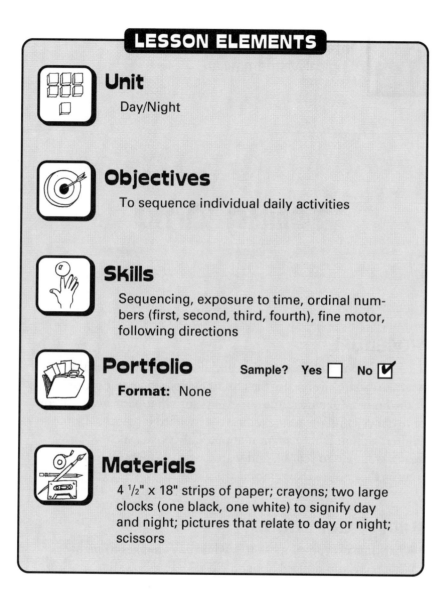

LESSON ELEMENTS

Unit
Day/Night

Objectives
To sequence individual daily activities

Skills
Sequencing, exposure to time, ordinal numbers (first, second, third, fourth), fine motor, following directions

Portfolio
Sample? Yes ☐ No ☑

Format: None

Materials
4 ½" x 18" strips of paper; crayons; two large clocks (one black, one white) to signify day and night; pictures that relate to day or night; scissors

COMMENTS

The children are given the option of either drawing four daytime activities, four nighttime activities, or two of each. Let children work in small groups to sequence each other's pictures.

Intelligence
Logical-Mathematical

Telling Time

PROCEDURE

Teach children about the minute and hour hand. Keeping the minute hand on twelve, let the children experiment with telling time on the hour. Make up stories or events for what happens each hour. Have children follow along telling time with their clocks. Let children volunteer information about daily events such as eating breakfast, going to school, and watching their favorite television show as they all set their clocks.

GUIDING QUESTIONS

- What time do you suppose it is when day changes to night?
- What have you noticed about a clock?
- How do you know what time to come to school?
- How do you know when to turn on your favorite TV show?

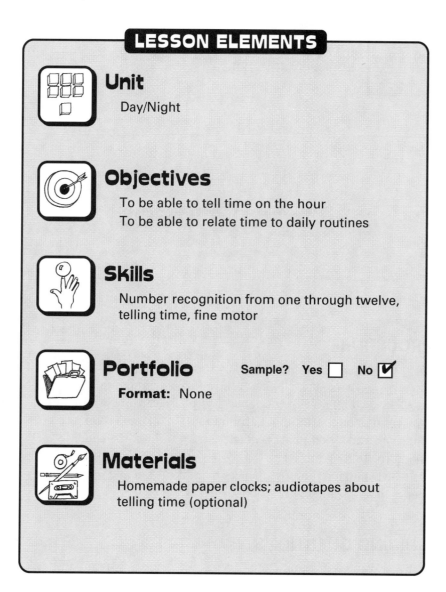

LESSON ELEMENTS

Unit
Day/Night

Objectives
To be able to tell time on the hour
To be able to relate time to daily routines

Skills
Number recognition from one through twelve, telling time, fine motor

Portfolio
Sample? Yes ☐ No ☑

Format: None

Materials
Homemade paper clocks; audiotapes about telling time (optional)

COMMENTS

Let children use their clocks to follow instructional records or audio-tapes about telling time. Children can also work in small groups to create stories and include the time each event takes place.

121

LIBRARY

Intelligence
Logical-Mathematical

Moon Phases

PROCEDURE

Introduce the sun and moon phase cards by asking children to identify the shape of each phase. Introduce any unfamiliar vocabulary. Have children help you label each phase card (new moon, crescent moon, quarter moon, full moon). In a large group, use pre-made sun and moon phase sequence strips and ask the children to take turns finding the shape that comes next. Let children create their own sun and moon sequences by putting sun and moon phase shapes in a repeating pattern on a strip of paper.

GUIDING QUESTIONS

- If you wanted to completely cover a sun shape how many full moons would you use?
- How many quarter moons would you use?
- What part of a full moon is a quarter moon?

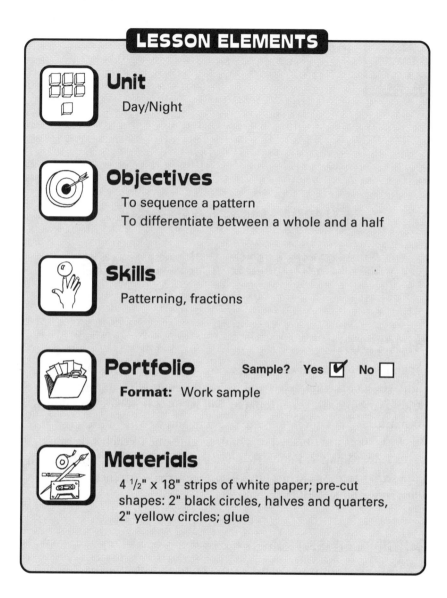

LESSON ELEMENTS

Unit
Day/Night

Objectives
To sequence a pattern
To differentiate between a whole and a half

Skills
Patterning, fractions

Portfolio
Sample? Yes ☑ No ☐
Format: Work sample

Materials
4 ¹/₂" x 18" strips of white paper; pre-cut shapes: 2" black circles, halves and quarters, 2" yellow circles; glue

COMMENTS

Make materials available in the math center for children to create border patterns on a 12" x 18" piece of construction paper to frame constellation pictures (see Lesson 51).

Intelligence
Spatial/Artistic

Day and Night Contrast Pictures

PROCEDURE

Let children tell about things they do and see during the day and night. Present the materials and ask children guiding questions. Let children decide which color paper will be used for chalk and which for markers. Let children create one day and one night picture. When pictures are finished let children glue one to each side of a larger colored paper. Punch two holes in the top of the "frame" and hang with yarn. As closure, share comments you overheard during work time and let children share their discoveries.

GUIDING QUESTIONS

- Why do you suppose we are using white and black paper?
- How are white and black paper alike or different from day and night?
- How do you think using chalk will be different from using markers?

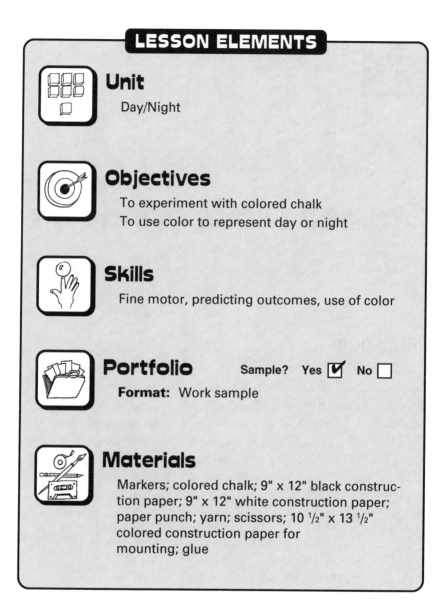

LESSON ELEMENTS

Unit
Day/Night

Objectives
To experiment with colored chalk
To use color to represent day or night

Skills
Fine motor, predicting outcomes, use of color

Portfolio
Sample? Yes ☑ No ☐
Format: Work sample

Materials
Markers; colored chalk; 9" x 12" black construction paper; 9" x 12" white construction paper; paper punch; yarn; scissors; 10 ½" x 13 ½" colored construction paper for mounting; glue

COMMENTS

Take note of discoveries being made as children experiment with materials. Smudging is a problem with chalk. You might want to demonstrate using a paper towel or scrap paper to cover work to avoid smudging.

Intelligence
Spatial/Artistic

Stained Glass Windows

PROCEDURE

Let children tell what they know about stained glass windows. Present pictures or samples, if possible. Let children observe and discuss colors, shapes, and dark and light elements of these samples. Demonstrate how to fold and cut designs out of paper. Guide children in making folds in the black paper and cutting shapes out of the paper. Let children glue tissue paper over holes. Tape stained glass creations to classroom windows. When all children's work is displayed, let children look at their stained glass windows and discuss designs, patterns, and effects of varied light conditions on their work.

GUIDING QUESTIONS

- How can we use these materials to make stained glass windows?
- How can we make holes in the black paper to let light through?
- What do you notice when you look at the tissue paper on the table?
- What do you notice when you hold the tissue paper up to the light?

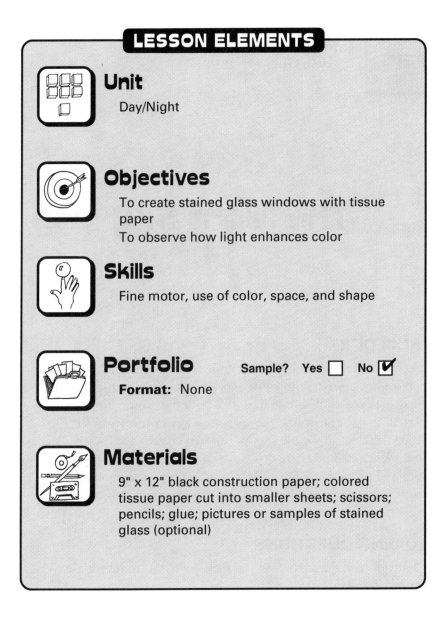

LESSON ELEMENTS

Unit
Day/Night

Objectives
To create stained glass windows with tissue paper
To observe how light enhances color

Skills
Fine motor, use of color, space, and shape

Portfolio   Sample? Yes ☐ No ☑
Format: None

Materials
9" x 12" black construction paper; colored tissue paper cut into smaller sheets; scissors; pencils; glue; pictures or samples of stained glass (optional)

COMMENTS
Note discoveries being made as children open folds and observe cut out shapes. Some children may want to draw shapes to cut out.

Intelligence
Spatial/Artistic

The Night Sky

PROCEDURE

Let children tell what they know about constellations, drawing on their knowledge from previous experiences. Using pictures of the constellations, ask children to notice both the position of the stars in relation to each other and the spaces between the stars in the Big Dipper. Present materials and let children create their own constellations. When paintings are dry, have children share their constellations and name them. Let children make additional observations about likenesses and differences they see in others' constellations.

GUIDING QUESTIONS

- How do you think you can use these materials to invent a new constellation?
- What objects made up of stars could you imagine seeing in the night sky?
- When you look at your constellation what does it remind you of? Why?

128

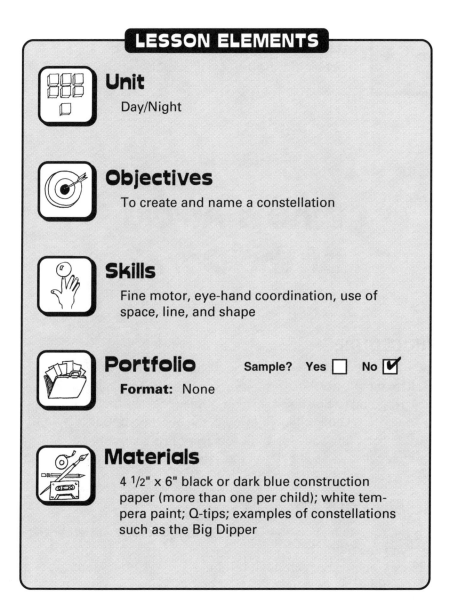

LESSON ELEMENTS

Unit
Day/Night

Objectives
To create and name a constellation

Skills
Fine motor, eye-hand coordination, use of space, line, and shape

Portfolio
Format: None

Sample? Yes ☐ No ☑

Materials
4 1/2" x 6" black or dark blue construction paper (more than one per child); white tempera paint; Q-tips; examples of constellations such as the Big Dipper

COMMENTS
Use library books such as *Find the Constellations* by H.A. Rey to expose children to constellations.

Intelligence
Inter- and Intrapersonal/Social

Who's Afraid of the Dark?

PROCEDURE

After reading children a story about being frightened, ask children to share their fears. After discussion time, explain to children that they are going to find a special light inside of themselves by listening to your voice. Guide children through the imagery of "Light Up the Dark." (See Comments for guided imagery.) As a closure, ask children what it was like to feel the light inside of themselves.

GUIDING QUESTIONS

- Is there anything you do to make yourself feel better or feel braver when you're afraid?
- Have you ever been afraid at bedtime?
- How did having the light inside of you make you feel?
- What can you tell us about someone you know who is afraid?
- How do you help people who are afraid?

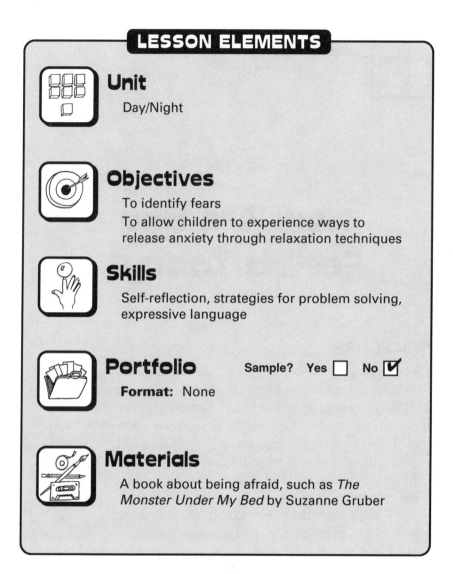

LESSON ELEMENTS

Unit
Day/Night

Objectives
To identify fears
To allow children to experience ways to
release anxiety through relaxation techniques

Skills
Self-reflection, strategies for problem solving,
expressive language

Portfolio   Sample? Yes ☐ No ☑
Format: None

Materials
A book about being afraid, such as *The
Monster Under My Bed* by Suzanne Gruber

COMMENTS

The teacher may choose to create his or her own guided imagery or
use the one provided. "Light Up the Dark": Begin with deep breathing exercises. While children focus on each breath, describe a gentle
summer scene at the beach or other familiar location with the sun
shining brightly. Suggest that each child has light inside him or her
that glows like the sun. Let children focus quietly on their own
special light using your voice and words as gentle guidance.

Intelligence
Inter- and Intrapersonal/Social

How Are You Feeling Today?

PROCEDURE

Before reading a story about feelings, ask children how day changes to night. As day changes to night so do feelings change. Let children use their own experiences to explain how their feelings have changed. Then read and discuss the story. After discussion, have children form a circle. Begin singing: "What are you feeling? How are you feeling? Tell us how you're feeling today." Roll a ball of yarn to a child, keeping hold of your end. The child responds by telling how he or she is feeling and what contributed to that feeling. Then the child holds the yarn and rolls the ball to another child. Continue until each child has had a turn, creating a yarn web. Then all children let go of their yarn by placing the part they are holding on the floor or rug. End by having the last child roll the yarn back to you. To close the lesson, children stand up, look at, and discuss the web design.

GUIDING QUESTIONS

- How do you feel on a warm, sunny day?
- Do you feel differently on a cold, dark, rainy night?
- Have you noticed any children in our group who feel alike?
- Can you explain what you've noticed?

132

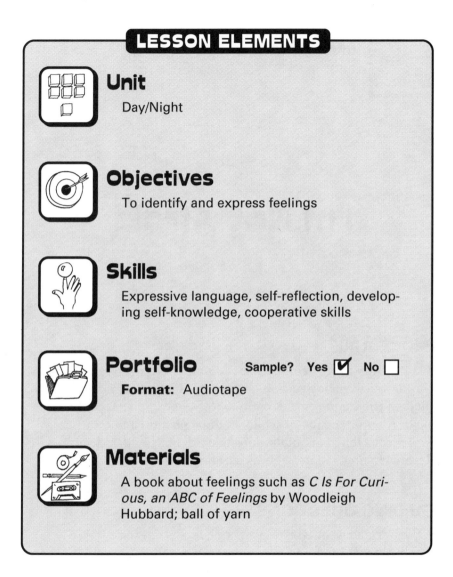

LESSON ELEMENTS

Unit
Day/Night

Objectives
To identify and express feelings

Skills
Expressive language, self-reflection, developing self-knowledge, cooperative skills

Portfolio Sample? Yes ☑ No ☐
Format: Audiotape

Materials
A book about feelings such as *C Is For Curious, an ABC of Feelings* by Woodleigh Hubbard; ball of yarn

COMMENTS

Children enjoy watching the changes in the web as the yarn is rolled back into a ball.

Intelligence
Inter- and Intrapersonal/Social

I'm Not Afraid

PROCEDURE

Read *It Didn't Frighten Me!* Use examples from the book to discuss illusion versus reality such as shadows that look like monsters. Let children cite examples of their own fears when going to bed at night. After discussion, let children draw pictures and create their own predictable book of illusions that "didn't frighten them." Record children's statements as text for the book.

GUIDING QUESTIONS

- What frightens or worries you at night?
- Why do you suppose that you feel this way?
- Do other people get afraid like you do? How do you know?

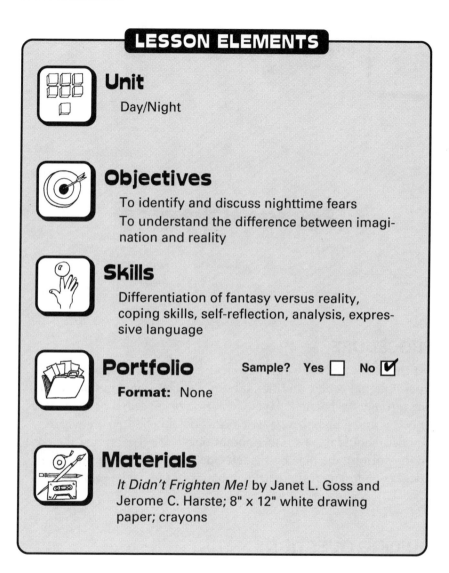

LESSON ELEMENTS

Unit
Day/Night

Objectives
To identify and discuss nighttime fears
To understand the difference between imagination and reality

Skills
Differentiation of fantasy versus reality, coping skills, self-reflection, analysis, expressive language

Portfolio   Sample? Yes ☐ No ☑
Format: None

Materials
It Didn't Frighten Me! by Janet L. Goss and Jerome C. Harste; 8" x 12" white drawing paper; crayons

COMMENTS

Make the classmade book available in the linguistic center. Let children who are interested share their book by "reading" to other adults and classes of children.

Intelligence
Spatial/Assembly

Paper Clocks

PROCEDURE

Let children observe a variety of clocks. Discuss differences among clocks (digital versus traditional face). Let children write numbers one through twelve on a paper clock face or on graph paper squares to be cut and glued on a paper clock. To help children see where numbers should be positioned, point out the twelve on top, the six on the bottom, the nine on the left side, and the three on the right side. Let children create their own hands or give them samples to trace, color, and cut.

GUIDING QUESTIONS

- How could we use these materials to help us make clocks?
- What do you notice about the numbers on the face of the clock?
- Why is it important to place the hands in the center of the clock?

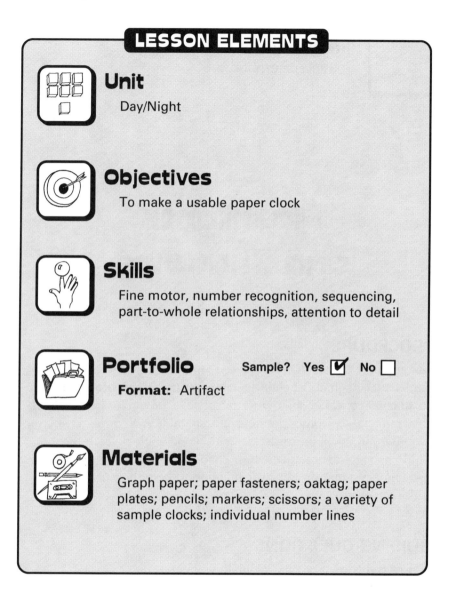

LESSON ELEMENTS

Unit
Day/Night

Objectives
To make a usable paper clock

Skills
Fine motor, number recognition, sequencing, part-to-whole relationships, attention to detail

Portfolio   Sample? Yes ☑ No ☐
Format: Artifact

Materials
Graph paper; paper fasteners; oaktag; paper plates; pencils; markers; scissors; a variety of sample clocks; individual number lines

COMMENTS
Use clocks to tell time on the hour and to tell time of daily activities (e.g., get up, go to school, eat lunch, go to bed, etc).

HOMEWORK
Ask children to count and record the number of clocks they have at home.

Intelligence
Spatial/Assembly

Flashlights
and Shadows

PROCEDURE

Ask children what they have noticed about shadows. Present disassembled flashlights. Let children tell what they know about the way flashlights work. Let children problem solve how to assemble them. Give minimal assistance, letting children guide each other. Display common objects (ball, stuffed animal, wooden block, etc.). Let children experiment with creating shadows that are long, short, big and little, and that disappear. Let children share their discoveries with each other.

GUIDING QUESTIONS

- How did you make this flashlight work?
- How can you make shadows change using a flashlight?
- How is a flashlight like the sun?

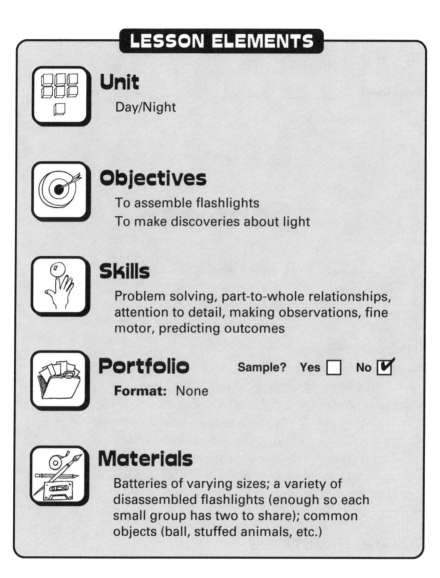

LESSON ELEMENTS

Unit
Day/Night

Objectives
To assemble flashlights
To make discoveries about light

Skills
Problem solving, part-to-whole relationships, attention to detail, making observations, fine motor, predicting outcomes

Portfolio
Sample? Yes ☐ No ☑
Format: None

Materials
Batteries of varying sizes; a variety of disassembled flashlights (enough so each small group has two to share); common objects (ball, stuffed animals, etc.)

COMMENTS

Leave disassembled flashlights and objects in the center for further investigation.

Intelligence
Spatial/Assembly

Candles

PROCEDURE

Introduce candles by asking children how they use candles in their homes. Present an example of a finished candle set in a cup filled with many layers of colored sand. Present materials and let children problem solve how the candle was made. As children tell what each of them needs and will do, write their directions on chart paper including pictures of the steps for younger children to follow. (See comments for candle making directions.) Let children work in pairs to help each other make candles.

GUIDING QUESTIONS

- How do you think this candle was made?
- Why do you think a partner is needed to make this project?
- What problems did you encounter making your candle? What was easiest for you?

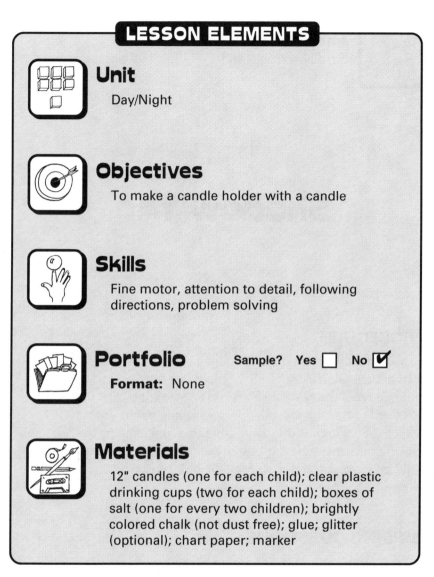

LESSON ELEMENTS

Unit
Day/Night

Objectives
To make a candle holder with a candle

Skills
Fine motor, attention to detail, following directions, problem solving

Portfolio
Sample? Yes ☐ No ☑
Format: None

Materials
12" candles (one for each child); clear plastic drinking cups (two for each child); boxes of salt (one for every two children); brightly colored chalk (not dust free); glue; glitter (optional); chart paper; marker

COMMENTS

Directions for candle making: One child holds a candle upright in a cup. Layers of colored salt are poured into the cup. (You can make colored salt ahead of time by rubbing chalk into small amounts of salt poured into extra cups.) When the cup is nearly full, children should pour glue into cup to form the top layer. The glue may be sprinkled with colored salt or glitter. Let glue dry overnight. The candles may be given as a gift.

141

Intelligence
Bodily-Kinesthetic

Shadow Tag

PROCEDURE

Explain the directions of the shadow tag game. (See comments for directions.) Ask children if they would like to play shadow tag. Let children retell the rules, then choose a "safe zone" like the shadow of the school or a tree outside. After playing by the given rules for a while, ask children if they have any ideas for changing the rules and making the game different or more fun. Play the game by the rules children suggest and discuss how the new rules worked or didn't work.

GUIDING QUESTIONS

- What could you do to keep from being tagged?
- What strategies do you think you could use if you are a shadow tagger?
- What rules would you change to make the game more fun?

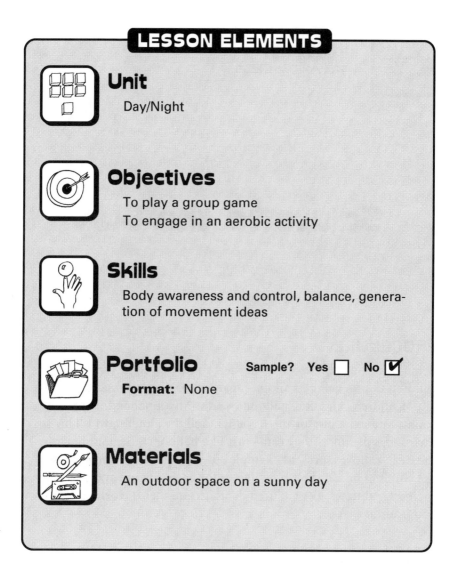

LESSON ELEMENTS

Unit
Day/Night

Objectives
To play a group game
To engage in an aerobic activity

Skills
Body awareness and control, balance, generation of movement ideas

Portfolio
Sample? Yes ☐ No ☑
Format: None

Materials
An outdoor space on a sunny day

COMMENTS

Shadow tag rules: Let one or more children be shadow taggers. When a tagger steps on another child's shadow, he or she is frozen until someone who is still mobile tags the frozen child's shadow. The "safe zone" is a designated shady place where no one's shadow can be seen and no one can be tagged.

Intelligence
Bodily-Kinesthetic

Salute to the Sun

PROCEDURE

Begin by asking children to find their space and to lie down. Guide children in practicing "balloon breaths," or diaphragmatic breathing. (Children can take "balloon breaths" by inhaling for three counts and exhaling for three counts. Tell the children to fill up their lungs as full as they can—just like balloons!) Beginning with the easiest moves, present examples of yoga postures one at a time. Let children invent their own names for each posture and practice each several times. Let children demonstrate their favorite postures and lead the class.

GUIDING QUESTIONS

- What does this posture look like to you?
- What part of your body can you feel stretching as you hold this posture?
- How do you feel when you take "balloon breaths"?

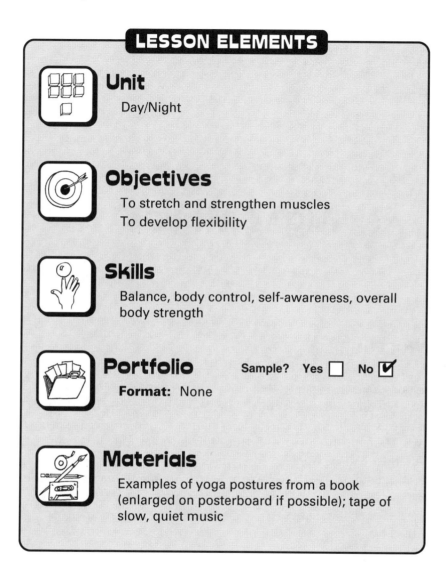

LESSON ELEMENTS

Unit
Day/Night

Objectives
To stretch and strengthen muscles
To develop flexibility

Skills
Balance, body control, self-awareness, overall body strength

Portfolio
Sample? Yes ☐ No ☑

Format: None

Materials
Examples of yoga postures from a book (enlarged on posterboard if possible); tape of slow, quiet music

COMMENTS

As children become more familiar with moves and more flexible with their bodies, you may introduce more difficult postures.

Intelligence
Bodily-Kinesthetic

Night Moves

PROCEDURE

Begin by brainstorming a list of "night things." Record children's responses on chart paper. Ask children to think about how these objects would move. Record children's responses including a variety of moves for the same object. Ask children to find a space of their own. Using the list generated, let children demonstrate night moves with their bodies. Guide children through level changes (low, middle, high) in using their space. Ask children to listen to the music and use some of the moves they have experimented with to create a dance. Let children use scarves. Play music with classroom lights turned off.

GUIDING QUESTIONS

- What kinds of things do you see, hear, and feel at night?
- How can you use your body to show stars twinkling (for example)?
- How can you show the moon rising (for example)?

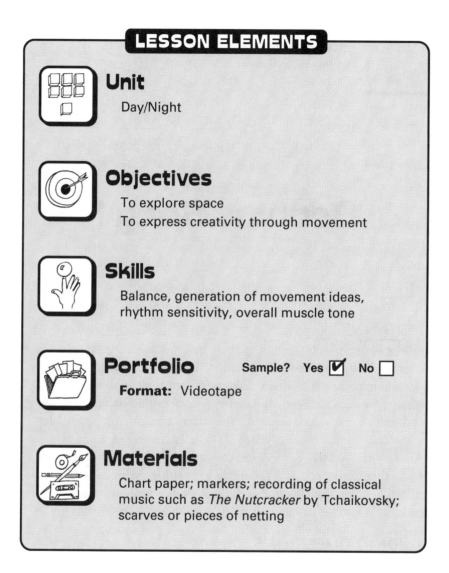

LESSON ELEMENTS

Unit
Day/Night

Objectives
To explore space
To express creativity through movement

Skills
Balance, generation of movement ideas, rhythm sensitivity, overall muscle tone

Portfolio
Sample? Yes ☑ No ☐
Format: Videotape

Materials
Chart paper; markers; recording of classical music such as *The Nutcracker* by Tchaikovsky; scarves or pieces of netting

COMMENTS

Netting sold by the yard in fabric stores is much less expensive than scarves. Cut netting into approximately two-foot squares. Children should have previous experience exploring scarves as props.

Intelligence
Musical

Bedtime Song I

PROCEDURE

After reading a bedtime story, discuss strategies children and adults use to help them get to sleep. Ask children if they would like to create their own bedtime alphabet song. Spread alphabet cards out randomly. Let children sequence the letters and glue them in order on the chart paper so each letter is at the beginning of a line followed by the words "is for." Let children complete each line. Turn on the tape recorder and let children experiment with melody and tempo. Let children sing the song in groups or individually.

GUIDING QUESTIONS

- How do you think the melody should sound?
- How would the tempo of the bedtime song affect the ability to fall asleep?
- How would the volume of our song affect the ability to fall asleep?

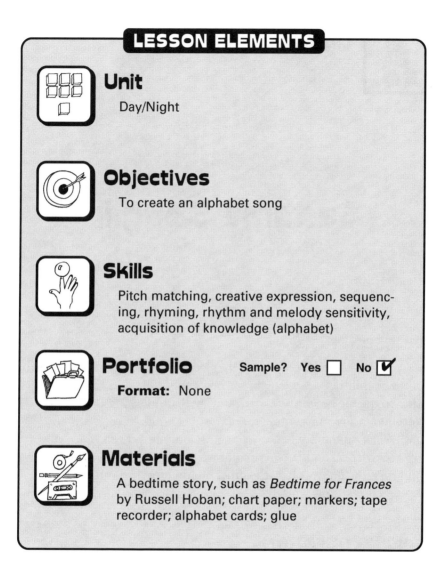

LESSON ELEMENTS

Unit
Day/Night

Objectives
To create an alphabet song

Skills
Pitch matching, creative expression, sequencing, rhyming, rhythm and melody sensitivity, acquisition of knowledge (alphabet)

Portfolio
Sample? Yes ☐ No ☑

Format: None

Materials
A bedtime story, such as *Bedtime for Frances* by Russell Hoban; chart paper; markers; tape recorder; alphabet cards; glue

COMMENTS
You may choose to assign homework for this lesson.

HOMEWORK
Make a copy of the song to send home with each child for singing at bedtime.

Intelligence
Musical

Bedtime Song II

PROCEDURE

Ask children to recall the events that led to their songwriting experience. Let children tell what they know about lullabies. Let children listen to the tape recording made during Bedtime Song I. Display instruments and ask guiding questions. Let children review their song, selecting times when instruments could be played. Turn the tape recorder on and let children practice singing and playing. Let a child rock the baby doll as the other children perform their completed bedtime song.

GUIDING QUESTIONS

- Do you think any of these instruments could be used during your song? For example, when you sing "R is for rabbit hopping through the grass," is there a way you could use an instrument to represent that rabbit hopping?
- How will the way you play your instrument affect the song?

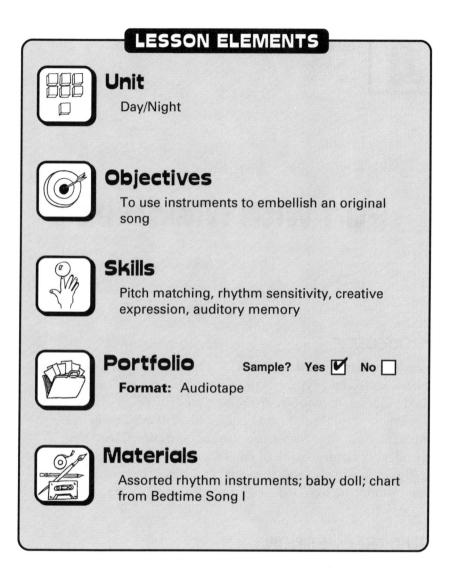

LESSON ELEMENTS

Unit
Day/Night

Objectives
To use instruments to embellish an original song

Skills
Pitch matching, rhythm sensitivity, creative expression, auditory memory

Portfolio   Sample? Yes ☑ No ☐
Format: Audiotape

Materials
Assorted rhythm instruments; baby doll; chart from Bedtime Song I

COMMENTS
Tape recordings should be made available for listening in the music center.

Intelligence
Musical

Fun with Melodies

PROCEDURE

Sing, then hum "Twinkle, Twinkle" a number of times, changing the tempo (speed), dynamics (loud, soft), and pitch. Teach the children different words to the same melody (e.g., "Twinkle, Twinkle," "Baa, Baa, Black Sheep," and "The ABC Song"). Let children invent their own words for the "Twinkle, Twinkle" melody. Let children work in pairs singing to each other and then in groups of four or six with one child at a time recording his or her song. Share tape recorded songs with the whole group.

GUIDING QUESTIONS

- Why does this tune sound familiar to you?
- Can you think of anything you would like to sing about?
- How could you use the "Twinkle, Twinkle" melody in your song?

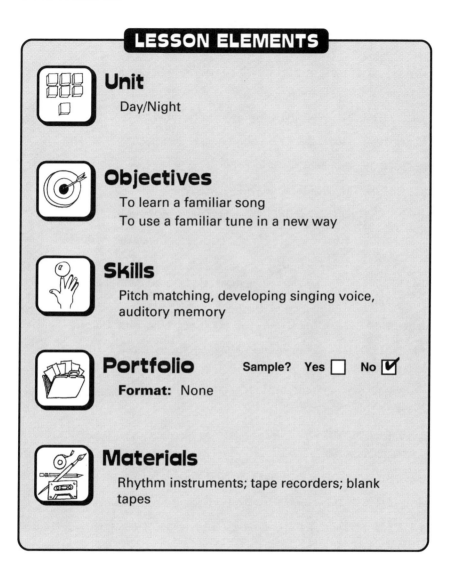

LESSON ELEMENTS

Unit
Day/Night

Objectives
To learn a familiar song
To use a familiar tune in a new way

Skills
Pitch matching, developing singing voice, auditory memory

Portfolio
Sample? Yes ☐ No ☑

Format: None

Materials
Rhythm instruments; tape recorders; blank tapes

COMMENTS

Let children use a tape recorder in the music center to hum and/or sing favorite songs in new ways. Let children share their tapes with classmates.

DAY/NIGHT UNIT BIBLIOGRAPHY

Arvetis, C., and Palmer, C. (1984). *What Makes Day and Night?* Middletown, Conn.: Field Publications.

Asch, F. (1993). *Moonbear.* New York: Simon & Schuster.

Asch, F. (1992). *Mooncake.* New York: Simon & Schuster.

Asch, F. (1985). *Bear Shadow.* New York: Simon & Schuster.

Asch, F. (1984). *Moongame.* New York: Simon & Schuster.

Berger, B. H. (1986). *Grandfather Twilight.* New York: Putnam.

Bolognese, E., and Bolognese, D. (1974). *The Sleepy Watchdog.* Pleasantville, N.Y.: Reader's Digest Services.

Bradbury, L. *Tell Me The Time.* Loughborough, Leicestershire, England: Ladybird Books.

Branley, F. M. (1987). *The Moon Seems to Change.* New York: HarperCollins.

Carle, E. (1991). *Papa, Please Get the Moon for Me.* Saxsonville, Mass.: Picture Book Studio.

Carlstron, N. W. (1992). *Who Gets the Sun Out of Bed?* Boston: Little Brown & Co.

Dayrell, E. (1990). *Why the Sun and the Moon Live in the Sky.* New York: Houghton Mifflin.

Dorros, A. (1990). *Me and My Shadow.* New York: Scholastic.

Ehlert, L. (1984). *Moon Rope.* New York: Harcourt Brace Jovanovich.

Goss, J. L., and Harste, J. C. (1985). *It Didn't Frighten Me!* St. Petersburg, Fla.: Willowisp Press.

Gruber, S. (1985). *The Monster Under My Bed.* Mahwah, N.J.: Troll Associates.

Hazbry, N. (1990). *How to Get Rid of Bad Dreams.* New York: Scholastic.

Hoban, R. (1960). *Bedtime for Frances.* New York: HarperCollins.

Hutchins, P. (1972). *Good-Night Owl.* New York: Macmillan Child Group.

Hort, L. (1991). *How Many Stars In The Sky?* New York: Morrow & Co.

Ipcar, D. (1967). *The Song of the Day Birds and the Night Birds.* Garden City, N.Y.: Doubleday.

Levinson, R. (1985). *Watch the Stars Come Out.* New York: E.P. Dutton.

Mayer, M. (1978). *Little Monster Bedtime Book.* New York: Golden Press.

Micicco, C. (1989). *A Little Night Music.* New York: Morrow.

Modesitt, J. (1989). *The Night Call.* New York: Viking Press.

Rey, H.A. (1962). *Find the Constellations.* Boston: Houghton Mifflin.

Rylant, C. (1991). *Night In The Country.* New York: Macmillan.

Saunders, S. (1987). *Mr. Nighttime and the Dream Machine.* New York: Scholastic.

Thurber, J. (1973). *Many Moons.* New York: Hartcourt, Brace, Jovanovich.

Viorst, J. (1972). *Alexander and the Terrible, Horrible, No Good, Very Bad Day.* New York: Macmillan.

Waber, B. (1972). *Ira Sleeps Over.* Boston: Houghton Mifflin.

Yolen, J. (1987). *Owl Moon.* New York: Scholastic.

Notes

Winter

The following unit, Winter, focuses on children's experiences with and knowledge of ice, snow, and cold as inspiration for creativity and exploration in the areas of multiple intelligences.

OBJECTIVES

- To make observations of winter
- To understand how winter affects people and animals
- To develop a sensitivity to the natural beauty of winter

WINTER UNIT OUTLINE

LINGUISTIC

The Snowy Day Children generate a list of snow activities and properties. After listening to *The Snowy Day* by Ezra Jack Keats, they compare their list to Peter's experiences.

Telling Winter Stories After the teacher tells a winter story from memory, children create their own versions. Children practice, then tape-record their stories.

Snow Poems After reading a variety of winter poems, children generate lists of sound, sight, and feeling words associated with snow and ice, then create their own winter poems.

LOGICAL-MATHEMATICAL

The Mitten After listening to a folktale, children organize information from the story by variables such as size and order.

Snowman Math Children demonstrate their knowledge of number operations using paper snowmen.

Winter Paths Children discover how to make paths on Geoboards and record their discoveries.

SPATIAL/ARTISTIC

Mosaic Snow People Children cooperate in creating giant snow people using small white paper squares.

A Winter's Day Children use an Epsom salt wash to create a frosted effect on an original crayon drawing.

Animals in Winter Children use magazine pictures of animals to create a winter habitat mural.

INTER- AND INTRAPERSONAL/SOCIAL

Winter Charade Children take turns pantomiming winter activities while peers try to identify the actions depicted.

Making Choices on a Winter Day I   Children choose from a variety of inexpensive objects. Children discuss and reflect on their decision-making process, then make their choices.

Making Choices on a Winter Day II   Children reflect on the choices they made and discuss the consequences of those choices.

SPATIAL/ASSEMBLY

Marshmallow Snow Shelters   Children use marshmallows and toothpicks to construct forts or houses.

Underground Sleepers   Children construct an underground diorama of hibernating animals using shoe boxes, socks, clay, etc.

Igloo Construction   Children assemble sugar cubes to make a model of an igloo.

BODILY-KINESTHETIC

Snow Fun   Children play follow the leader, make angels in the snow, and create their own snow fun.

Freeze Tag   A "snowman" tags children who become "ice sculptures."

Body Sculptures   Children take turns as the "sculptor" and the "block of ice" being molded.

MUSICAL

The Jacket I Wear in the Snow   Children act out a story and add sound effects.

Winter Poetic Sounds   Children use musical instruments to "decorate" original winter poems.

Winter Duets   Children use xylophones to create musical conversations to accompany a winter snowfall.

VOCABULARY

This vocabulary list includes language that is used in the lessons for this unit. At the beginning of a lesson you can introduce key words and ask the children to define them and present materials for labeling. Language that you have introduced and that children have generated is used throughout a lesson. After a lesson let children re-evaluate their definitions and clarify meaning for themselves.

boots
charades
choice
duet
footprints
frost
frozen
habitat
hibernate
ice cracking
ice house
ice sculpture
igloo

melt
mitten
non-verbal communication
pantomime
scarf
sculptor
shoveling
skater
sledding
snow angels
tunnel
warm

Unit: Winter
Lesson Plans

Intelligence
Linguistic

The Snowy Day

PROCEDURE

Let children tell about a snowy winter day they remember and record their experiences and observations with a red marker. After listening to Ezra Jack Keat's *The Snowy Day,* let children recall Peter's experiences and record their responses with blue marker. Help children compare their list of experiences to the one generated by *The Snowy Day.* Use a green marker to highlight experiences that the children and Peter had in common.

GUIDING QUESTIONS

- What kinds of things do you like to do on a snowy winter day?
- What words would you use to describe the snow you played in?
- What words on our chart make you feel cold?

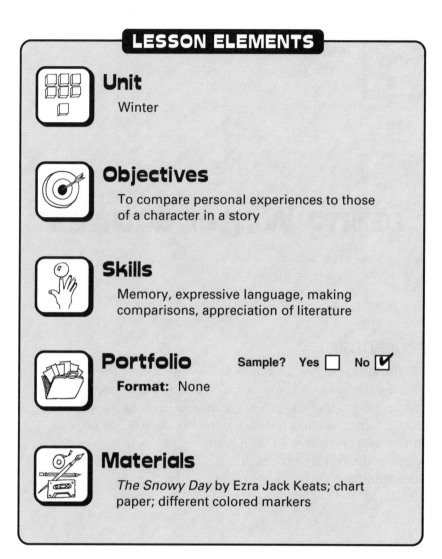

LESSON ELEMENTS

Unit
Winter

Objectives
To compare personal experiences to those of a character in a story

Skills
Memory, expressive language, making comparisons, appreciation of literature

Portfolio
Sample? Yes ☐ No ☑

Format: None

Materials
The Snowy Day by Ezra Jack Keats; chart paper; different colored markers

COMMENTS

Children may want to record events according to where they take place, inside or outside.

Intelligence
Linguistic

Telling Winter Stories

PROCEDURE

Tell the story. Discuss the events of the story and let the children retell the sequence using felt board figures. Focus on each character's dialogue and emotional motivation for language and actions. Let a few children take turns pretending to be one of the characters. Let children work in groups of four, each pretending to be one of the characters. Classroom objects may be used as the need for props arises. Each group retells the story in its own way as a miniplay.

GUIDING QUESTIONS

- How could we act out this story?
- What would you say if you were (one of the characters)?
- What kind of voice would a _____ have?
- How would _____ 's voice be different?

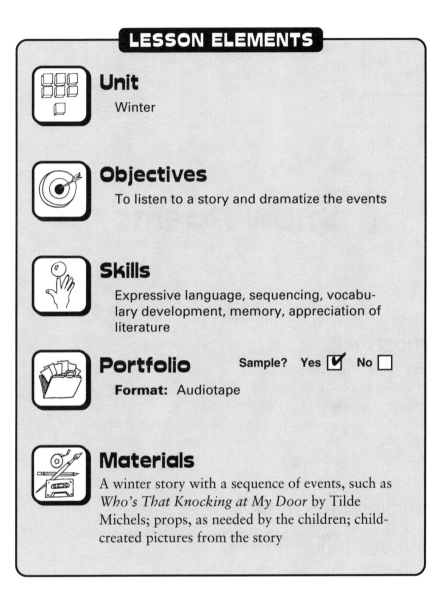

LESSON ELEMENTS

Unit
Winter

Objectives
To listen to a story and dramatize the events

Skills
Expressive language, sequencing, vocabulary development, memory, appreciation of literature

Portfolio
Sample? Yes ☑ No ☐

Format: Audiotape

Materials
A winter story with a sequence of events, such as *Who's That Knocking at My Door* by Tilde Michels; props, as needed by the children; child-created pictures from the story

COMMENTS
Children may need coaching in order to sound and move like the animal they represent.

Intelligence
Linguistic

Snow Poems

PROCEDURE

After observing a snowfall or going on a winter walk, read a variety of winter poems. Let children tell which words in the poems evoke images and feelings. Let children generate a list of winter words. Record their suggestions on chart paper. Use words from their list to generate ideas for poems and write one or more group poems with each child contributing a line.

GUIDING QUESTIONS

- How would you finish this sentence "the air was as cold as. . . ."? "the snow was like. . . "?
- What do icicles remind you of?
- What words mean the same as the word "cold" to you?

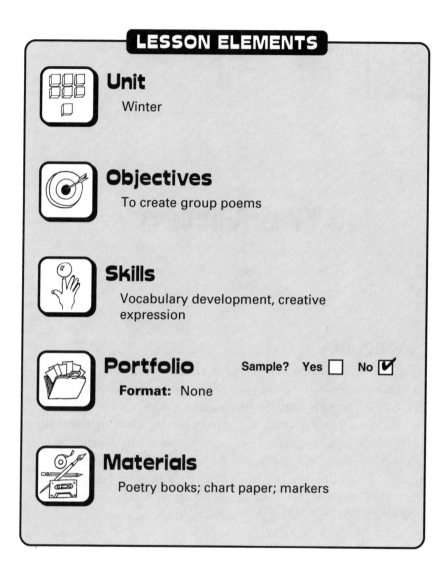

LESSON ELEMENTS

Unit
Winter

Objectives
To create group poems

Skills
Vocabulary development, creative expression

Portfolio   Sample?   Yes ☐   No ☑
Format: None

Materials
Poetry books; chart paper; markers

COMMENTS

You may use art and color to enhance the poems. For example, children may choose "snow" as a focus for one poem. You may choose to write the original poem on light blue, green, or lavender paper using "cool" colored markers and display with traditional snowflake art cut from square white paper.

Intelligence
Logical-Mathematical

The Mitten

PROCEDURE

Tell the folktale *The Mitten* using the animal pictures and a large paper mitten. Have the children arrange the animals in order of their entrance into the mitten (first, second, third, middle, last, etc.) Let children arrange animals in different ways such as by size (tall, taller, tallest, smallest, etc.). Continue to arrange the animals by different variables and features of the animals (2 feet, 4 feet, feathers, etc.). Let children retell the story in their own way as classmates guess what variable they have chosen, such as starting with the smallest animal and ending with the largest animal.

GUIDING QUESTIONS

- How do you suppose we're going to use this mitten and these animals?
- What are some other ways you could arrange the animals?
- What order (variables) do you think _____ used when telling the story?

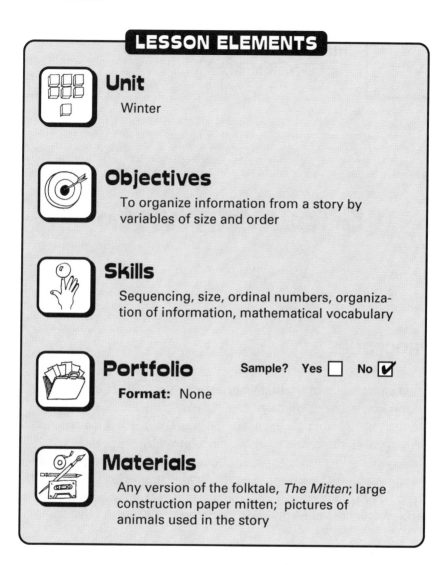

LESSON ELEMENTS

Unit
Winter

Objectives
To organize information from a story by variables of size and order

Skills
Sequencing, size, ordinal numbers, organization of information, mathematical vocabulary

Portfolio
Sample? Yes ☐ No ☑

Format: None

Materials
Any version of the folktale, *The Mitten*; large construction paper mitten; pictures of animals used in the story

COMMENTS
Place a variety of objects in the math center and have children discover ways of organizing them.

Intelligence
Logical-Mathematical

Snowman Math

PROCEDURE

Present the snowmen to the children and ask them to look carefully, noting differences in detail. Divide children into two teams. If there is an odd number of children use one scorer, if there's an even number, use a scorer for each team. Alternating between teams, ask each member a question. (See questions provided on page 172.) Scorers should record the number of correct responses. At the end of the questioning, the scorers should tally the number of correct responses for each team. Use a spinner to determine whether the team with more or less points is the winner.

GUIDING QUESTIONS

- What do you notice about these snowmen?
- What's the same about some of the snowmen?
- What kind of questions would you ask about the snowmen?

170

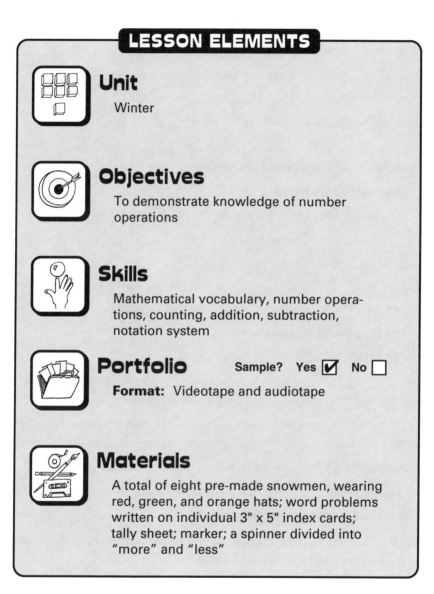

LESSON ELEMENTS

Unit
Winter

Objectives
To demonstrate knowledge of number operations

Skills
Mathematical vocabulary, number operations, counting, addition, subtraction, notation system

Portfolio
Sample? Yes ☑ No ☐
Format: Videotape and audiotape

Materials
A total of eight pre-made snowmen, wearing red, green, and orange hats; word problems written on individual 3" x 5" index cards; tally sheet; marker; a spinner divided into "more" and "less"

COMMENTS
In the math center children can create their own word problems by working in pairs. They can also record the problems by dictating them onto a tape recorder.

SNOWMAN QUESTIONS

How many snowmen are on the rug?

How many snowmen have red hats?

How many snowmen have green hats?

How many snowmen are there with both red and green hats?

There were five little snowmen short and fat, each one wearing a funny hat. The sun melted one. How many are left?

___ snowmen have red hats.

___ snowmen have green hats.

___ snowmen have orange hats.

How many different color hats are there?

(child's name) built three snowmen. (child's name) came and built one more. How many snowmen are there all together?

Count the number of snowmen.

Count backwards.

girl, girl, girl, and boy built a snowman. (Use children's names in the spaces.) How many boys built a snowman? girls? children?

There were five snowmen. Four of them got knocked down. How many were left?

When you count the snowmen, what number follows three?

When you count the snowmen, what number comes after seven?

When you count the snowmen, what number comes before five?

These snowmen are standing in a row. What color hat does the first snowman have on? the third? the fifth?

UNIT: WINTER

Intelligence
Logical-Mathematical

Winter Paths

PROCEDURE

Ask the children, "What happens when you walk in the snow? How would you be able to find a friend who was hiding?" Generate discussion about footprints in paths. Divide children into pairs and give each pair a Geoboard. Children take turns putting a red cube on the top left-hand nail and a green cube on the bottom right-hand nail and making a path from the "red house" to the "green house" with a Geoband. Children try as many ways as possible to connect the two "houses."

GUIDING QUESTIONS

- How can you use Geobands to connect the two houses?
- Can you explain how you get from one place to another?
- Why do you think it is important for the ends of the Geoband to over lap on the nail?

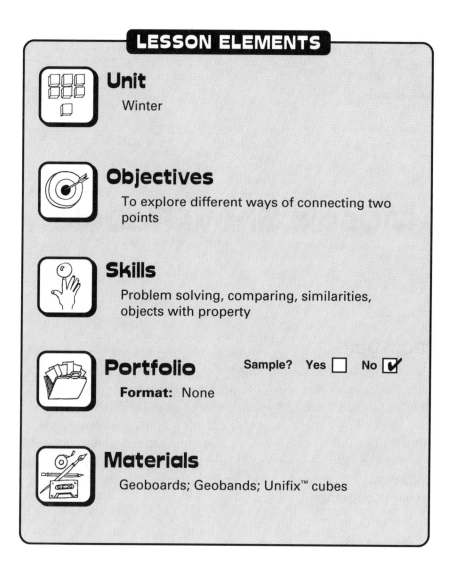

LESSON ELEMENTS

Unit
Winter

Objectives
To explore different ways of connecting two points

Skills
Problem solving, comparing, similarities, objects with property

Portfolio
Format: None

Sample? Yes ☐ No ☑

Materials
Geoboards; Geobands; Unifix™ cubes

COMMENTS

The children may want to record the different paths on Geoboard dot paper.

Intelligence
Spatial/Artistic

Mosaic Snow People

PROCEDURE

Ask children to describe the shape of a snow person. With their help, draw the outline of a snow person on large craft paper. Ask children to describe the color of a snow person. Display 1 $^1/_2$" squares of white paper. Using glue, let a few children show how to fill in the outline. Display pictures of mosaic art. Ask children to compare the examples they made with the mosaic pictures. Let children work together to fill in the snow person's body and add details with squares of colored paper.

GUIDING QUESTIONS

- How could you use these white paper squares to make a snow person?
- What color paper squares could you use for the snowman's nose? mouth? hat? buttons?
- What do you notice about this mosaic picture?

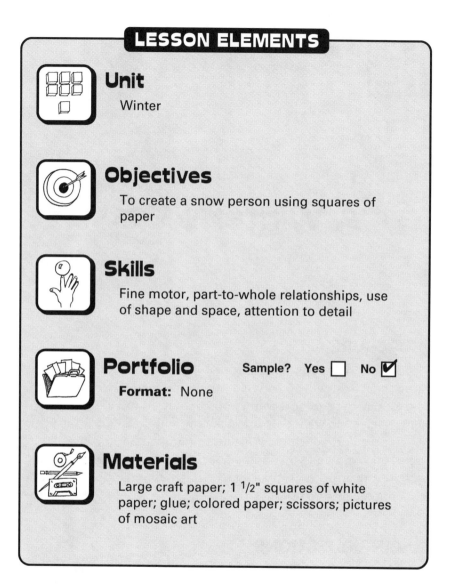

LESSON ELEMENTS

Unit
Winter

Objectives
To create a snow person using squares of paper

Skills
Fine motor, part-to-whole relationships, use of shape and space, attention to detail

Portfolio
Sample? Yes ☐ No ☑

Format: None

Materials
Large craft paper; 1 1/2" squares of white paper; glue; colored paper; scissors; pictures of mosaic art

COMMENTS

Children will want to make their snow person a man or a woman and give it a name.

HOMEWORK

Use the mosaic technique to create a picture at home.

Intelligence
Spatial/Artistic

A Winter's Day

PROCEDURE

Display materials and tell children they will make a frosty picture but that the frost will go on last as an overall wash. Tell children to imagine that they are in a warm house looking outside on a cold winter's day. Ask what they see. Ask how they could draw the scene and give it color. Let children make their drawings using lots of color. When drawings are finished, let children brush an Epsom salt wash over their pictures. Explain to children that the frost cannot be seen until the picture dries.

GUIDING QUESTIONS

- How can you use crayons to make very strong, bright colors?
- What colors do you think will look best on blue paper?
- How do you think the picture will look different when the Epsom salt wash dries?

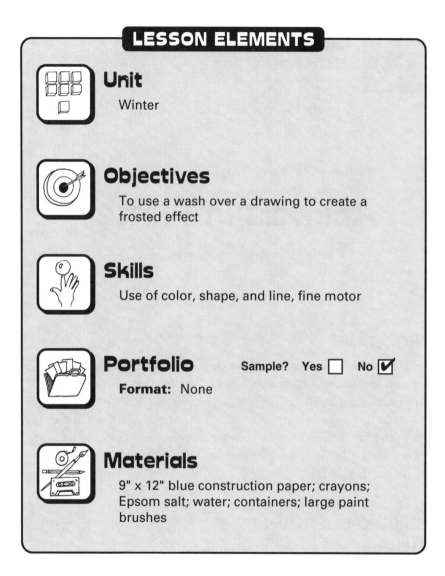

LESSON ELEMENTS

Unit
Winter

Objectives
To use a wash over a drawing to create a frosted effect

Skills
Use of color, shape, and line, fine motor

Portfolio
Format: None

Sample? Yes ☐ No ☑

Materials
9" x 12" blue construction paper; crayons; Epsom salt; water; containers; large paint brushes

COMMENTS

This lesson could be used as a follow-up to Lesson 64.

Wash recipe: One part warm water to one part Epsom salt (do not skimp). Use a large brush to apply a thick coating. Be sure to check the paper before you use it in class; some types do not wash well.

Intelligence
Spatial/Artistic

Animals in Winter

PROCEDURE

Display animal pictures. Let children tell what they know about specific animals and their habitats. Let each child choose one animal picture, cut it out, and place it on a piece of paper. Ask each child to tell what he or she will draw to depict the animal's winter home. Let children glue their pictures and begin drawing and coloring habitat scenes. To close the lesson, let children place pictures together on the floor for all to see.

GUIDING QUESTIONS

- How can you show where this animal lives?
- What colors will you use to create your animal's habitat?
- How will someone who looks at your picture know that it's winter?

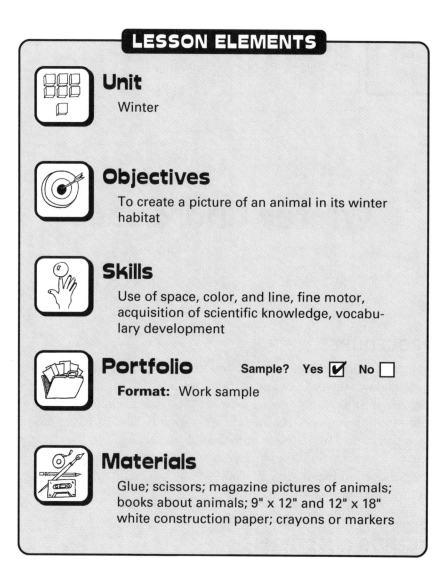

LESSON ELEMENTS

Unit
Winter

Objectives
To create a picture of an animal in its winter habitat

Skills
Use of space, color, and line, fine motor, acquisition of scientific knowledge, vocabulary development

Portfolio
Sample? Yes ☑ No ☐

Format: Work sample

Materials
Glue; scissors; magazine pictures of animals; books about animals; 9" x 12" and 12" x 18" white construction paper; crayons or markers

COMMENTS

Children should have previous knowledge of animals that hibernate, migrate, and stay in local habitat during winter season.

Intelligence
Inter- and Intrapersonal/Social

Winter Charades

PROCEDURE

Ask children how they can make you think something by using their body and not their voice. Let children demonstrate examples. Divide children into pairs. Ask one child from each pair to choose a pantomime card. Whisper to the two children what their card says. Let each pair of children demonstrate the action as the group tries to identify the activity. Have children who are performing say "begin" and "finish" so the observing group will be respectful and attentive to the performers.

GUIDING QUESTIONS

- How can you tell something without using words?
- How do your friends use their bodies and their faces to show you they are mad?
- What other ways have you noticed your friends communicating nonverbally?

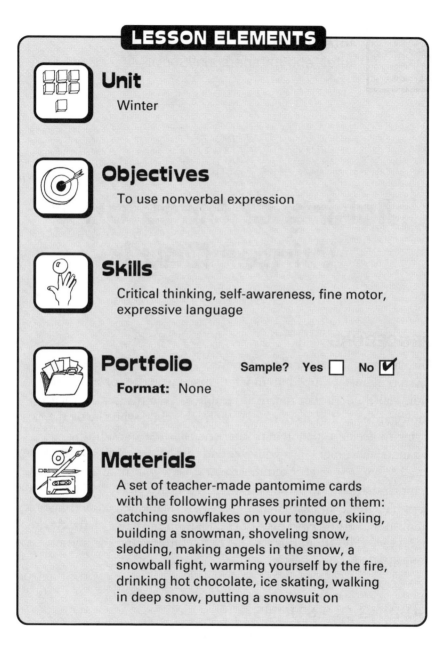

LESSON ELEMENTS

Unit
Winter

Objectives
To use nonverbal expression

Skills
Critical thinking, self-awareness, fine motor, expressive language

Portfolio
Format: None

Sample? Yes ☐ No ☑

Materials
A set of teacher-made pantomime cards with the following phrases printed on them: catching snowflakes on your tongue, skiing, building a snowman, shoveling snow, sledding, making angels in the snow, a snowball fight, warming yourself by the fire, drinking hot chocolate, ice skating, walking in deep snow, putting a snowsuit on

COMMENTS

Make drawing paper and markers available in the social center. Children can draw winter objects such as a snowman and create their own set of cards to play charades with their peers.

Intelligence
Inter- and Intrapersonal/Social

74

Making Choices on a Winter Day I

PROCEDURE

Display three items—a dime-store item, an edible item, and a mystery item—wrapped up in white tissue paper to form a snowball. Tell children that they will be able to keep the item of their choice at the end of the lesson. Coach each child while he or she is trying to decide which item to choose. Ask these questions to facilitate choosing: Have you ever had this before? Will it last a long time? What is special about this to you? Can you share it? Do you want to share it? How can you use it? Ask each child to make his or her final choice and explain why he or she made that choice. Each child should also record his or her choice on the name chart. At the end, every child should receive his or her choice, and the mystery item should be revealed.

GUIDING QUESTIONS

- Which item do you think you would like and why?
- Why do you suppose (name) chose the mystery item?
- Why do you think (name) chose the food item?

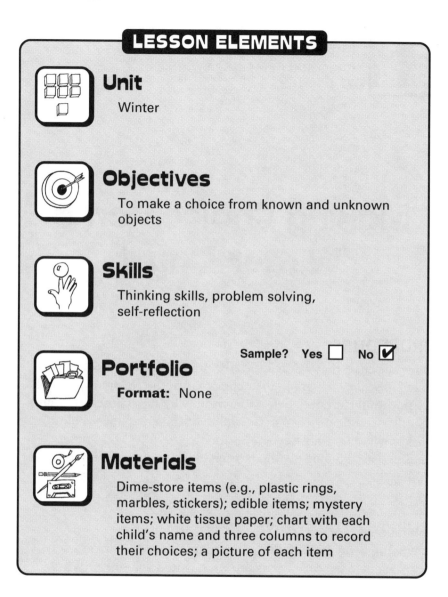

LESSON ELEMENTS

Unit
Winter

Objectives
To make a choice from known and unknown objects

Skills
Thinking skills, problem solving, self-reflection

Portfolio
Sample? Yes ☐ No ☑

Format: None

Materials
Dime-store items (e.g., plastic rings, marbles, stickers); edible items; mystery items; white tissue paper; chart with each child's name and three columns to record their choices; a picture of each item

COMMENTS

Children will want to talk about whether they think the mystery item was more or less desirable than the known items. Some children may not be happy with the mystery item. You may want to end one day with this lesson and begin the next day with Lesson 75.

Intelligence
Inter- and Intrapersonal/Social

Making Choices on a Winter Day II

PROCEDURE

Show the chart that was made in the previous lesson. Ask each child to tell how they felt about their choices. Ask the children who took a risk with the mystery object to explain why they chose something that they could not see. Ask the children who chose the visible objects why they didn't choose the mystery object. Make observations and ask guiding questions as children continue to discuss their choices.

GUIDING QUESTIONS

- What did you think of the choice that you made?
- If you could choose over again, what would you select? Why?
- What did you learn from your choice?
- Why do you think (name) is unhappy with his or her choice?
- What do you think (name) will do the next time he or she has a choice to make?

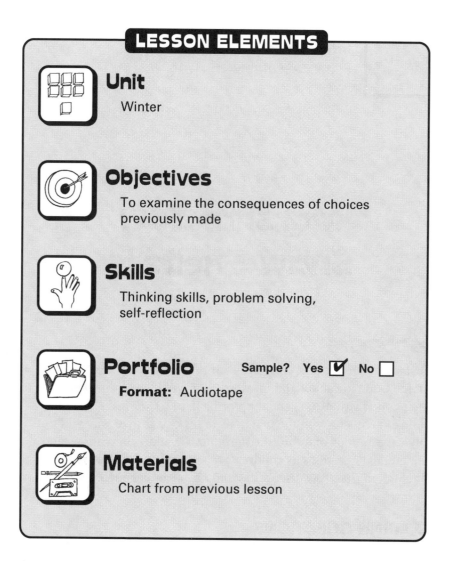

LESSON ELEMENTS

Unit
Winter

Objectives
To examine the consequences of choices previously made

Skills
Thinking skills, problem solving, self-reflection

Portfolio
Sample? Yes ☑ No ☐
Format: Audiotape

Materials
Chart from previous lesson

COMMENTS

To validate children's choices the teacher might want to repeat children's responses in a positive way. For example, you might say, "John says he prefers to know what he's getting. Mary says she likes surprises." By stating the children's reactions in a positive way, you show the children that their choices and feelings are valued.

Audiotapes can be transcribed with individual children's comments placed in their portfolios.

Intelligence
Spatial/Assembly

Marshmallow Snow Shelters

PROCEDURE

Display materials. Ask children what they think they are going to make. Compare snow and marshmallows. Ask children whether their constructions will stand up or be flat (2-D or 3-D). Let each child experiment with the materials in his or her own way without any expectations of a "finished product." Make observations and ask guiding questions as children problem solve. To close the lesson, let children share the discoveries and problems encountered.

GUIDING QUESTIONS

- How are marshmallows like snow?
- How can you use these materials to make a house with walls and a roof?
- How will you be able to support the roof?

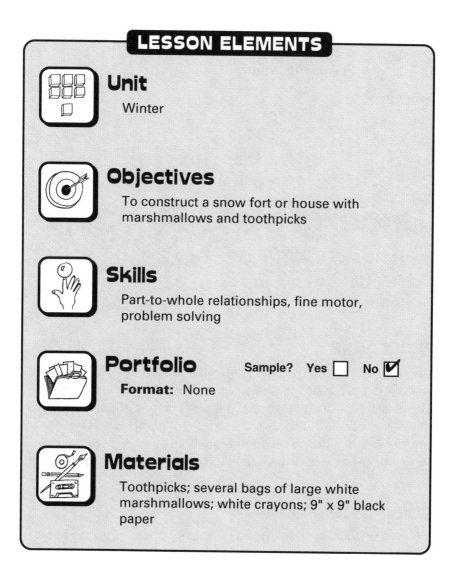

LESSON ELEMENTS

Unit
Winter

Objectives
To construct a snow fort or house with marshmallows and toothpicks

Skills
Part-to-whole relationships, fine motor, problem solving

Portfolio
Sample? Yes ☐ No ☑

Format: None

Materials
Toothpicks; several bags of large white marshmallows; white crayons; 9" x 9" black paper

COMMENTS

Save one marshmallow for each child to eat after the lesson.

Display snow shelter constructions in a wintery scene. You may want to take notes or photograph some of the constructions.

Provide materials in a spatial/assembly center for further exploration. Children will probably want more time to explore these materials.

Intelligence
Spatial/Assembly

Underground Sleepers

PROCEDURE

Display pictures of hibernating animals and discuss children's observations. Display materials. Let children predict how they will use the materials including techniques for creating animals with clay. Let children create dioramas with sock tunnels and clay animals to inhabit them. When dioramas are complete let children show and describe how their animal lives in winter.

GUIDING QUESTIONS

- How can you use these materials to make an underground home for a hibernating animal?
- What parts do you think might be difficult for you?
- How could a friend or an adult help you?

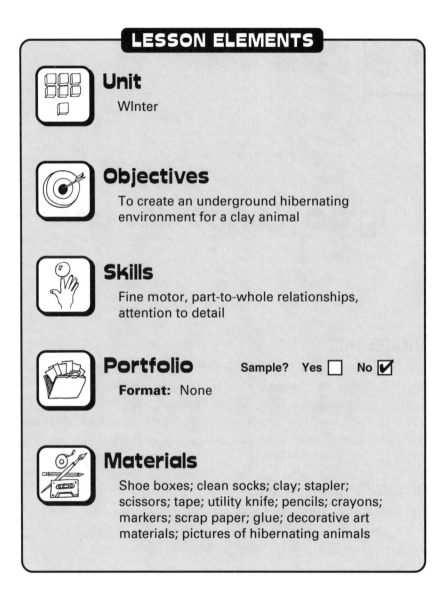

LESSON ELEMENTS

Unit
WInter

Objectives
To create an underground hibernating environment for a clay animal

Skills
Fine motor, part-to-whole relationships, attention to detail

Portfolio
Sample? Yes ☐ No ☑
Format: None

Materials
Shoe boxes; clean socks; clay; stapler; scissors; tape; utility knife; pencils; crayons; markers; scrap paper; glue; decorative art materials; pictures of hibernating animals

COMMENTS

The teacher assists children in making holes in boxes by circulating with a utility knife. Children may work in pairs to help each other before asking the teacher for help.

Intelligence
Spatial/Assembly

Igloo Construction

PROCEDURE

Let children work in pairs without glue to plan their construction. Let children practice balancing sugar cubes. Allow time for experimenting and problem solving until children are ready to use glue. When children have had ample time to plan and experiment, present glue and pieces of cardboard for construction of final product.

GUIDING QUESTIONS

- How can these materials be used to construct an igloo?
- What are some ways you could make the walls? the roof?
- What are some ideas you have for keeping the structure together?

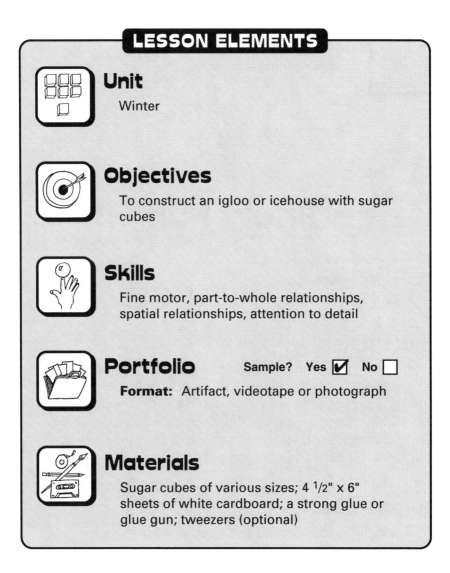

LESSON ELEMENTS

Unit
Winter

Objectives
To construct an igloo or icehouse with sugar cubes

Skills
Fine motor, part-to-whole relationships, spatial relationships, attention to detail

Portfolio
Sample? Yes ☑ No ☐

Format: Artifact, videotape or photograph

Materials
Sugar cubes of various sizes; 4 1/2" x 6" sheets of white cardboard; a strong glue or glue gun; tweezers (optional)

COMMENTS

Display igloos on a white tablecloth or sheet and let children add other elements to the winter scene.

You will need to experiment with different types of adhesives to find what works best. Water-based adhesives do not work well with sugar cubes.

Intelligence
Bodily-Kinesthetic

Snow Fun

PROCEDURE

Help children dress appropriately to go outside after a snowfall. Let children play "follow the leader," stepping in each other's footprints. Let each child have an oppurtunity to be the leader and create a unique way of walking. Encourage children to make "angels in the snow" and roll snow into balls to form snowmen. Let children create their own snow games.

GUIDING QUESTIONS

- What kinds of impressions can you make in the snow with your body?
- How can you tell your footprints from those of others?
- How do you walk differently when snow is on the ground?

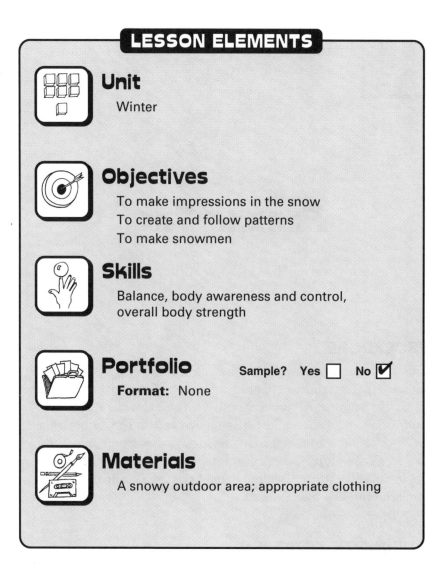

LESSON ELEMENTS

Unit
Winter

Objectives
To make impressions in the snow
To create and follow patterns
To make snowmen

Skills
Balance, body awareness and control, overall body strength

Portfolio
Sample? Yes ☐ No ☑
Format: None

Materials
A snowy outdoor area; appropriate clothing

COMMENTS

In anticipation of this snowy day activity, children may want to collect materials for decorating their snowmen.

If you live in an area where snow does not fall, sprinkle baby powder on the floor for making tracks and make lots of white playdough for children to use for snowmen. Shaving cream on table tops can be used for making finger patterns. Have a "Snow Falls in Our Class Day"!

Intelligence
Bodily-Kinesthetic

Freeze Tag

PROCEDURE

This activity can be played in a large open room or outside on a snowy day. Let children establish a "safe area" and give it a winter name like "snow fort" or "icehouse." Let one child be the "snowman" who chases "the skaters" who are in danger on "thin ice." Any child who is tagged by the snowman is frozen in position like an ice sculpture. Skaters may bring the ice sculptures back to life by touching them. Children in the "safe area" cannot be frozen into sculptures by the "snowman."

GUIDING QUESTIONS

- What strategies could you use as the snowman? as a skater?
- How could you change the rules of this game to make it more fun?
- How can you use this timer as part of the game?

196

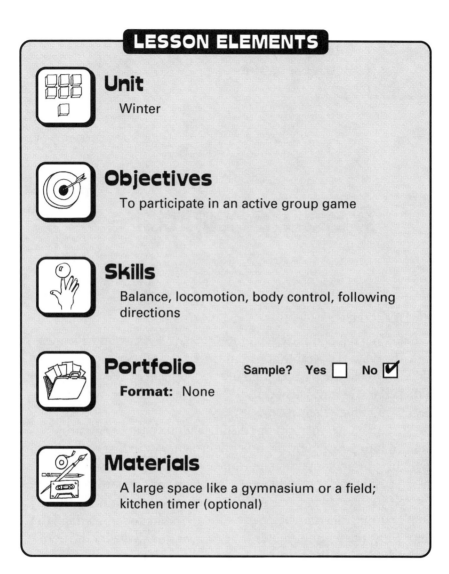

LESSON ELEMENTS

Unit
Winter

Objectives
To participate in an active group game

Skills
Balance, locomotion, body control, following directions

Portfolio
Format: None

Sample? Yes ☐ No ☑

Materials
A large space like a gymnasium or a field; kitchen timer (optional)

COMMENTS

After playing by one set of rules, display a timer and let children create new rules incorporating the timer. Play the variations that children invent and compare them.

Intelligence
Bodily-Kinesthetic

Body Sculptures

PROCEDURE

Let children tell about ice sculptures they have seen and have them describe what the sculptor does and what the block of ice does. Ask children to choose partners and decide who will be the ice and who will be the sculptor. Demonstrate "gentle molding," before students begin "molding" their partners.

First standing, then sitting, then lying, one partner is gently molded into position by the other. During the standing sculpture, give cues for making "final adjustments." Ask sculptors to walk around and look at the different "ice sculptures" before they return to their partners. The same sculptor then molds his or her partner who is sitting this time. Repeat walking around and observing. The third time, the sculptor molds his or her partner lying on the floor. Have children change roles and repeat the molding process. As closure, ask how each pair of children worked together, including both problems and positive aspects.

GUIDING QUESTIONS

- Which job did you like better, being the ice or the sculptor? Why?
- What kinds of small changes can you make in your sculpture?
- How does the sculpture make you feel?
- Why do you think you feel that way?

198

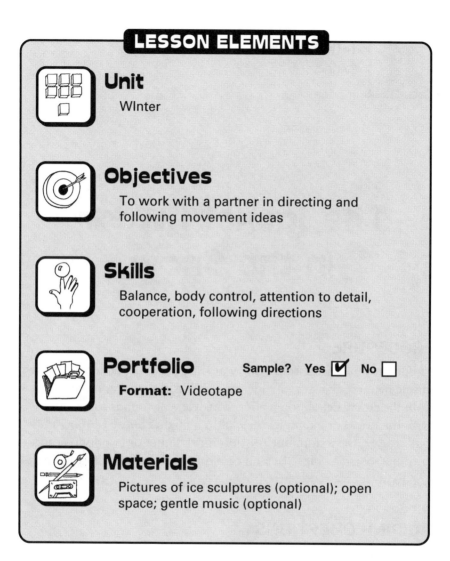

LESSON ELEMENTS

Unit
WInter

Objectives
To work with a partner in directing and following movement ideas

Skills
Balance, body control, attention to detail, cooperation, following directions

Portfolio   Sample? Yes ☑ No ☐
Format: Videotape

Materials
Pictures of ice sculptures (optional); open space; gentle music (optional)

COMMENTS

Before students choose partners, ask children to think carefully about who works well with them, will listen, and will cooperate.

Videotaping children provides opportunities to assess individuals' sense of balance, ability to hold position, overall body strength, generation of ideas, cooperation, and level of interest.

Intelligence
Musical

The Jacket I Wear in the Snow

PROCEDURE

Children should listen to the story at least once. Let children review the elements of the story by identifying and sequencing pictures from the story. Let children choose instrument sounds to accompany the text. For example, the children might choose running the mallet along the xylophone for the zipper sound or two loud gongs for the "boots too big." Reread the story with individuals adding sounds at appropriate parts.

GUIDING QUESTIONS

- Which instrument do you suppose could make a sound that feels like an itchy sweater? like boots that are too big?
- How could you use an instrument to sound like tears dripping?
- How could you make the sound of the jacket's zipper?

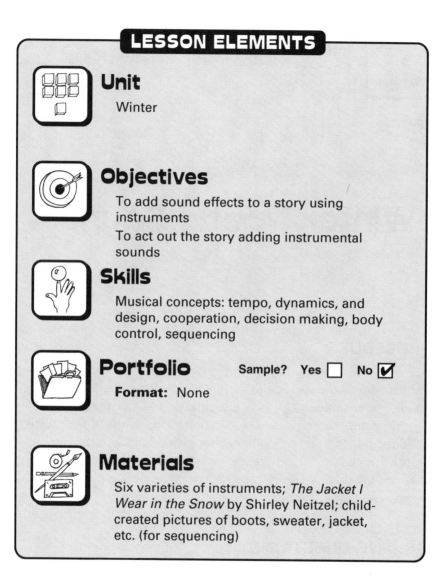

LESSON ELEMENTS

Unit
Winter

Objectives
To add sound effects to a story using instruments

To act out the story adding instrumental sounds

Skills
Musical concepts: tempo, dynamics, and design, cooperation, decision making, body control, sequencing

Portfolio
Sample? Yes ☐ No ☑

Format: None

Materials
Six varieties of instruments; *The Jacket I Wear in the Snow* by Shirley Neitzel; child-created pictures of boots, sweater, jacket, etc. (for sequencing)

COMMENTS

Let children devise ways to represent or notate their musical choices on pictures of objects from the book. For example, two large dots may stand for the two loud gongs for the "boots too big."

Intelligence
Musical

Winter Poetic Sounds

PROCEDURE

Begin by reading some poems previously generated by groups or individuals. (You may choose to use published children's poems about winter subjects.) Display instruments and let children decide how instruments can be used to "decorate" the words of the poems. Read the poems as a few children with instruments accompany the words. Let children comment on accompaniments and suggest changes. Let other children experiment with adding instrumental sounds and repeat discussion about musical choices.

GUIDING QUESTIONS

- Do any of the words in the poems remind you of any sounds these instruments make?
- How would you play your instrument to go with (insert words or phrases such as "snow falling" or "ice cracking")?

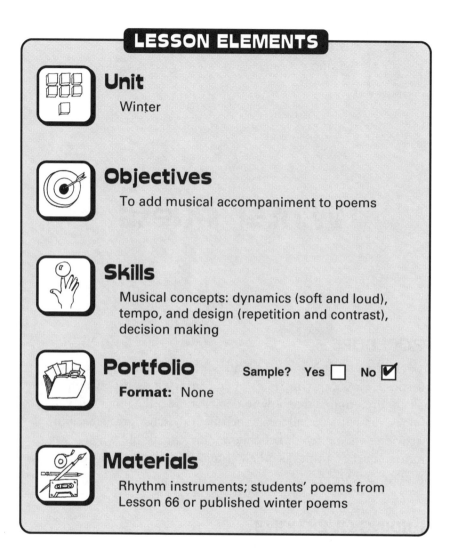

LESSON ELEMENTS

Unit
Winter

Objectives
To add musical accompaniment to poems

Skills
Musical concepts: dynamics (soft and loud), tempo, and design (repetition and contrast), decision making

Portfolio
Sample? Yes ☐ No ☑

Format: None

Materials
Rhythm instruments; students' poems from Lesson 66 or published winter poems

COMMENTS

Write a few favorite winter poems or chants on chart paper and place them in the music center for additional exploration with instrumental accompaniments.

Intelligence
Musical

Winter Duets

PROCEDURE

Ask children to sit in pairs and talk with one another. Ask this question: How can you "play" a conversation on the xylophone? Ask children to imagine how to depict snow falling on their xylophones. Let pairs of children experiment. Discuss problems and discoveries encountered. Let children play duets and when ready, tape one duet at a time as others listen. As a closure, play back tape for all to enjoy.

GUIDING QUESTIONS

- How could you play the xylophone with a friend?
- How could you "play" a conversation on the xylophone?
- What ideas do you have for cooperating during your musical conversation?

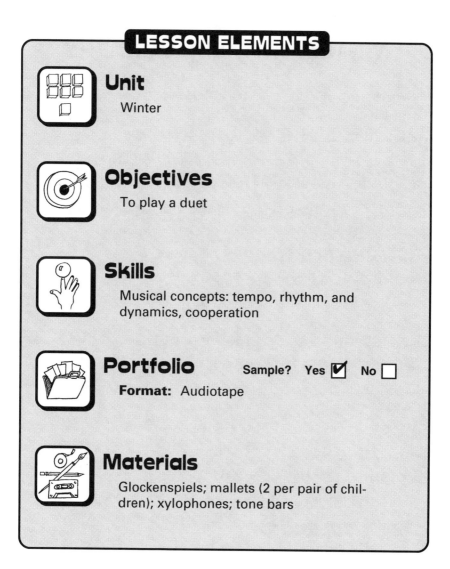

LESSON ELEMENTS

Unit
Winter

Objectives
To play a duet

Skills
Musical concepts: tempo, rhythm, and dynamics, cooperation

Portfolio
Sample? Yes ☑ No ☐

Format: Audiotape

Materials
Glockenspiels; mallets (2 per pair of children); xylophones; tone bars

COMMENTS

Children will discover that instruments are capable of more than one sound, but are best at one or two. Let children decide which group these instruments belong with.

WINTER UNIT BIBLIOGRAPHY

Bancroft, H., and VanGelder, R. G. (1963). *Animals In Winter*. New York: Scholastic.

Borden, L. (1992). *Caps, Hats, Socks and Mittens*. New York: Scholastic.

Burton, V. L. (1973). *Katy and the Big Snow*. Boston: Houghton Mifflin.

Craft, R. (1975). *Winter Bear*. New York: Macmillan.

Gretz, S. (1985). *Teddy Bears Cure a Cold*. New York: Macmillan.

Hader, B., and Hader, E. (1988). *Big Snow*. New York: Macmillan.

Keats, E. J. (1962). *The Snowy Day*. New York: Penguin.

Keller, H. (1988). *Geraldine's Big Snow*. New York: Greenwillow Books.

Kellogg, S. (1979). *The Mystery of the Missing Red Mitten*. New York: Dial Books.

Littledale, F. (1989). *The Snow Child*. New York: Scholastic.

Michels, T. (1986). *Who's That Knocking at My Door?* New York: Barron.

Neitzel, S. (1989). *The Jacket I Wear in the Snow*. New York: Greenwillow Books.

Tejima, K. (1987). *Fox's Dream*. New York: Putnam.

Thayer, J. (1986). *The Puppy Who Wanted a Boy*. New York: Morrow.

Tresselt, A. (1989). *The Mitten*. New York: Morrow.

Tresselt, A. (1989). *White Snow, Bright Snow*. New York: Lothrop.

Yolen, J. (1987). *Owl Moon*. New York: Putnam.

Zolotow, C. (1972). *Hold My Hand*. New York: HarperCollins.

Castles

The following unit, Castles, focuses on exploring the facts and fantasies of medieval times.

OBJECTIVES

- To develop knowledge of fairy tales
- To develop an understanding of the structure and purpose of a castle
- To be exposed to medieval life and times

CASTLES UNIT OUTLINE

 LINGUISTIC

Creating a Fairy Tale   Using props, children brainstorm characters and actions and develop a story.

King Midas   After listening to the story, children create their own story about something turning into gold.

Fairy Tales   After hearing two favorite fairy tales, students compare similarities and differences in characters and plots using a Venn diagram.

LOGICAL-MATHEMATICAL

One Hundred Stone Castles   In pairs, children estimate how many rolls of a die it takes to reach one hundred and use a graph paper castle to record their findings.

Castle Counting   Children make a castle and count, record, and graph the number of blocks used.

Coins and Jewels   Children explore quantity by estimating collections of objects in jars by counting and making comparisons.

SPATIAL/ARTISTIC

Create a Dragon   Using a variety of materials, small groups work together to create and assemble dragons.

Clay Dragons   Children explore the use of clay in creating three-dimensional dragons.

Sand Castles   Children use sand, paper, and glue to create a textured castle drawing.

 INTER- AND INTRAPERSONAL/SOCIAL

The Dragon   After reading a story, children discuss showing off, being frightened, and being left out.

The Princess and the Pea   After hearing the story, children identify personality traits and differences among the characters and use
props to re-enact the story.

Dragon Emotions   Children discuss different emotions exhibited
by dragons in pictures and stories. They use original art work to
characterize their dragons.

 SPATIAL/ASSEMBLY

Building a Classroom Castle   Children construct a large cardboard classroom castle to play in.

Building Castles in Small Groups   Children use blocks to construct castles with specific architectural challenges.

Weapons   Children design and construct swords and shields.

 BODILY-KINESTHETIC

The King and the Dragon   After listening to a story, children
identify characters and their actions and retell the story adding their
own physical interpretations.

Move Like a Dragon   After discussing different types of dragons
and how they would move, children create group dragons and move
to a variety of musical pieces.

Tournament of Knights   Children use homemade swords and
shields to demonstrate their strength.

♫ **MUSICAL**

Old King Glory   Children learn a cooperative action song and
improvise sound effects for a story about a prince.

The Generous Dragon   Children participate in a cumulative story
adding sound effects, keeping the beat, and building to a crescendo.

The Little Prince   Children explore the use of voices in creating
castle sound effects and in singing a repetitive song.

VOCABULARY

This vocabulary list includes language that is used in the lessons for this unit. At the beginning of a lesson you can introduce key words and ask the children to define them and present materials for labeling. Language that you have introduced and that children have generated is used throughout a lesson. After a lesson let children re-evaluate their definitions and clarify meaning for themselves.

across	prop
armor	queen
battlements	scales
castle	scoop
castle keep	shield
chain	sword
character	tally
clumsy	terrain
cooperate	texture
crenelated	tournament
crescendo	walls
dice	weapon
die	
drawbridge	
dungeon	
fairy tale	
greedy	
jester	
joust	
king	
knight	
lonely	
mall	
medieval tower	
moat	
obstacle	
page	
plot	
prince	
princess	

Unit: Castles
Lesson Plans

Intelligence
Linguistic

Creating a Fairy Tale

PROCEDURE

Let children brainstorm characters for a fairy tale while you record suggestions. Write "once upon a time" at the top of the easel paper and "they lived happily ever after" at the bottom. Have children give directions as to how the story develops by creating a problem for their charachter to solve. Children designated as characters will dramatize the story as other children dictate it. Let children choose props for their characters. Once the story is complete, let all children take turns acting it out in small groups for the class.

GUIDING QUESTIONS

- How does a fairy tale usually begin? end?
- What magical events can take place in a fairy tale?
- What are some ways our story's problem could be solved?

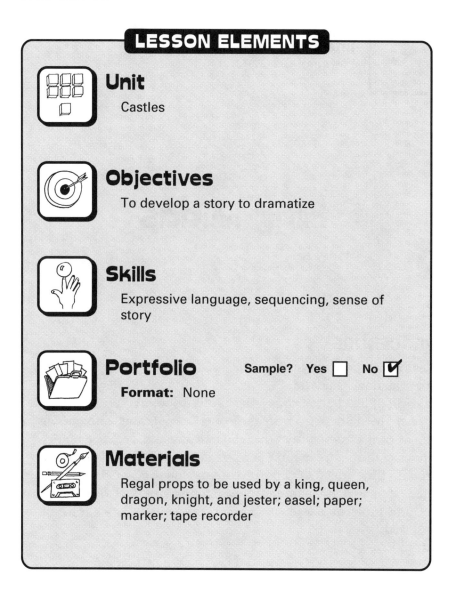

LESSON ELEMENTS

Unit
Castles

Objectives
To develop a story to dramatize

Skills
Expressive language, sequencing, sense of story

Portfolio
Sample? Yes ☐ No ☑

Format: None

Materials
Regal props to be used by a king, queen, dragon, knight, and jester; easel; paper; marker; tape recorder

COMMENTS

Children enjoy creating their own stories in pairs or in small groups and recording them on audiotape.

Intelligence
Linguistic

King Midas

PROCEDURE

Read or tell the story of *King Midas*. Discuss the events of the story stressing how King Midas was granted one wish. Review the consequences of his choice and how his problems were resolved.

Ask the children to create their own story starting with one wish. Brainstorm a list of wishes that children might make. Let children illustrate their story in three parts. Ask each child to tell his or her story to three friends and tape record the final version. In their illustrations, children are encouraged to think of their wish first, then the problem that the wish creates, and finally, how the problem is solved.

GUIDING QUESTIONS

- If you were granted one wish, what would you wish for? Why?
- What kinds of things could happen as a result of your choice?
- How would your story end?

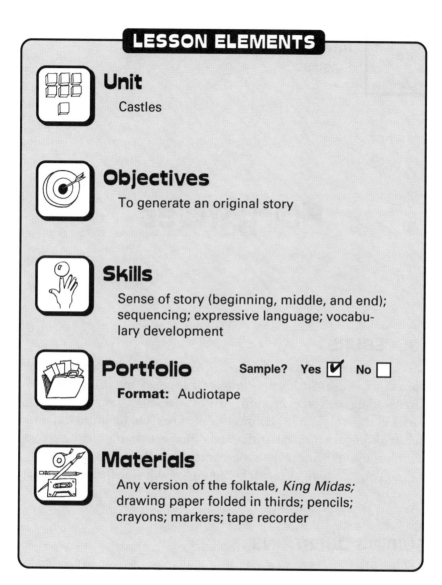

LESSON ELEMENTS

Unit
Castles

Objectives
To generate an original story

Skills
Sense of story (beginning, middle, and end); sequencing; expressive language; vocabulary development

Portfolio   Sample? Yes ☑ No ☐
Format: Audiotape

Materials
Any version of the folktale, *King Midas;* drawing paper folded in thirds; pencils; crayons; markers; tape recorder

COMMENTS

A parent volunteer can be asked to transcribe the tape. Stories can be printed from a computer and pictures can be added.

Intelligence
Linguistic

Fairy Tales

PROCEDURE

This lesson takes three days to complete. On different days the
stories of *Rumplestiltskin* and *Rapunzel* are read and discussed.
After reading each story, record a list of characters, problems, and
events in the story, and solutions or outcomes. On the third day, let
children compare the similarities and differences in the characters
and plots using their previously generated list. Record responses on
a Venn diagram with elements common to both stories in the center.

GUIDING QUESTIONS

- How do you think Rapunzel's stepmother and Rumplestiltskin are
  alike?
- How did the story of *Rumplestiltskin* end differently from
  Rapunzel?
- Which fairy tale was your favorite? Why?

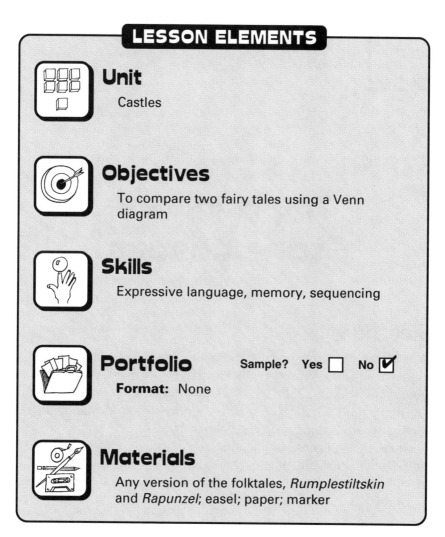

LESSON ELEMENTS

Unit
Castles

Objectives
To compare two fairy tales using a Venn diagram

Skills
Expressive language, memory, sequencing

Portfolio
Sample? Yes ☐ No ☑

Format: None

Materials
Any version of the folktales, *Rumplestiltskin* and *Rapunzel*; easel; paper; marker

COMMENTS

A Venn diagram is useful for comparing and contrasting.

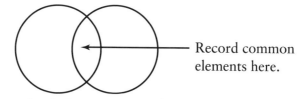

Record common elements here.

Rumplestiltskin   *Rapunzel*

Intelligence
Logical-Mathematical

One Hundred Stone Castles

PROCEDURE

Demonstrate throwing one die and counting as many blocks on the graph paper as the number on the die. If a six is rolled, count six squares and make an X on the sixth square. Ask children to estimate how many times the die will be thrown to reach the one hundredth square. Record responses on easel paper. Have one child at a time throw the die and continue counting and marking until one hundred is reached. Tally the number of times the die was thrown. Record the amount and compare it with the previous estimates. You may repeat this several times and compare results.

GUIDING QUESTIONS

- What is the lowest number you can roll when you throw a die? the highest number?
- How many rolls of the die do you think it will take to make one hundred? Why?

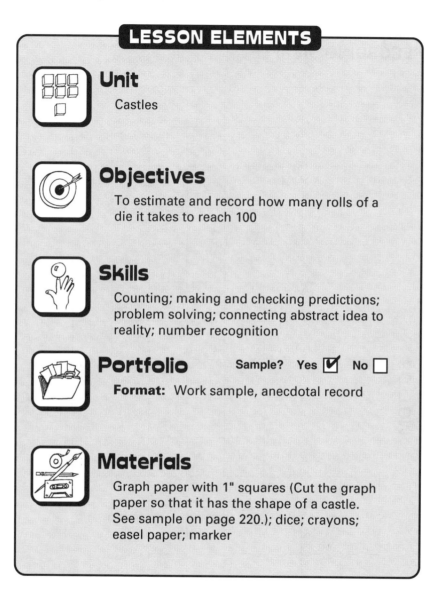

LESSON ELEMENTS

Unit
Castles

Objectives
To estimate and record how many rolls of a die it takes to reach 100

Skills
Counting; making and checking predictions; problem solving; connecting abstract idea to reality; number recognition

Portfolio
Sample? Yes ☑ No ☐

Format: Work sample, anecdotal record

Materials
Graph paper with 1" squares (Cut the graph paper so that it has the shape of a castle. See sample on page 220.); dice; crayons; easel paper; marker

COMMENTS

Let children repeat the lesson in pairs. Each pair decides who will tally and who will throw the die.

ONE HUNDRED STONE CASTLES
RECORDING SAMPLE

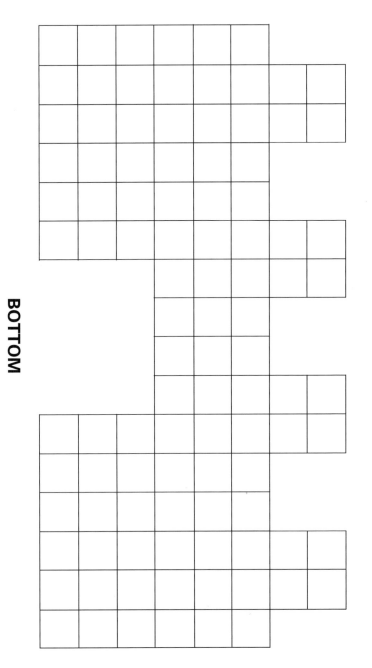

BOTTOM

TOP

UNIT: CASTLES

Intelligence
Logical-Mathematical

Castle Counting

PROCEDURE

Give each child a game board. (Sample on page 225.) Read the spatial directions and let children use the visual and auditory clues to color in a castle on the game board. (Directions on page 224.) On the following day, divide children into pairs and ask them to make a castle using graph paper. Have them count, record, and graph the number of blocks they used to make their castle. Let pairs of children display their original graph paper castles and explain how they created them.

GUIDING QUESTIONS

- What are castles made of?
- How many stones do you think are used to construct a castle?
- Are all castles the same size?
- What makes them different?

222

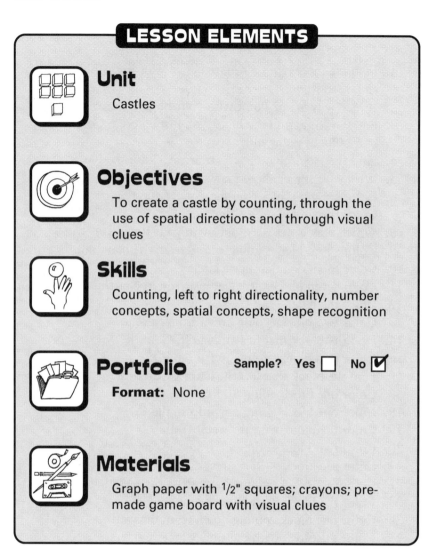

LESSON ELEMENTS

Unit
Castles

Objectives
To create a castle by counting, through the use of spatial directions and through visual clues

Skills
Counting, left to right directionality, number concepts, spatial concepts, shape recognition

Portfolio
Sample? Yes ☐   No ☑

Format: None

Materials
Graph paper with 1/2" squares; crayons; pre-made game board with visual clues

COMMENTS

Make graph paper available in the math center. Let children draw other objects and count how many squares make up the area of each.

DIRECTIONS

1. Find the block with a square in it. Color in the block with a square in it.
2. Which way is up? Point with your finger.
3. Put your finger on the block you just colored. Color six more blocks going up.
4. Find the block that has the triangle. Color the block.
5. With your finger show me which way is down.
6. Color six more blocks going down from the triangle.
7. Color the square with a diamond.
8. Which way is across? Point with your finger.
9. Color seven blocks going across from the diamond.
10. Color the block that has a circle.
11. Color seven blocks going across from the circle.
12. Color the block with the star in it.
13. Color two blocks going down from the star.
14. Find the block that has an X in it. Color it.
15. Color two blocks going up from the X.
16. Find the block that has the letter C. Color it.
17. Color one block going up from the C.
18. Color one block going down from the C.
19. Color the block with the number one.
20. Color two blocks going up from the one.
21. Color the block with the rectangle.
22. Color two blocks going down from the rectangle.
23. Color the block with an oval in it.
24. Color one block coming down from the oval.
25. Color the block with the smiley face.
26. Going across from the smiley face, skip one block and color the next block, then skip one more block and color the next block after that.

What has appeared on your paper?

CASTLE COUNTING GAMEBOARD

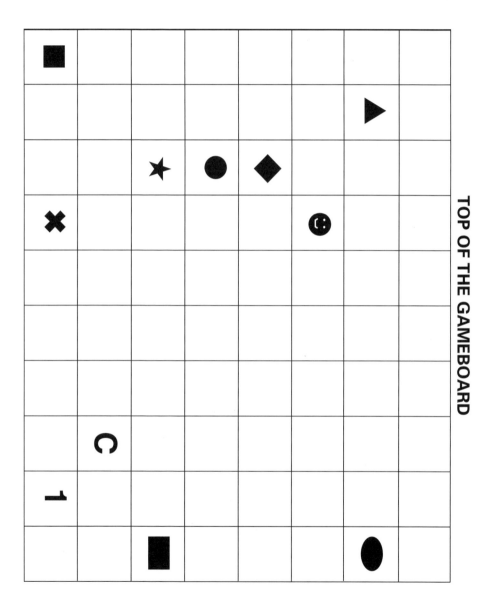

TOP OF THE GAMEBOARD

Intelligence
Logical-Mathematical

Coins and Jewels

PROCEDURE

Fill one small jar with coins. Present a second jar of a different size. Ask the children whether the second jar can hold more or less coins or the same amount. Fill the second jar with coins. Check by counting the coins in each jar.

Have children predict how many scoops of jewels it will take to fill a jar. Check. Present a larger scoop. Ask children to predict how many scoops of jewels will fill the same jar now. Let children use paper and markers to tally the number of scoops needed. Repeat using a different size jar with the same sized scoop. After many different demonstrations and observations, let children work in small groups to estimate, count, tally, and record using a variety of materials.

GUIDING QUESTIONS

- How many scoops of jewels do you think it will take to fill this jar? How can you find out?
- Which jar has more coins, tiles, stones? What makes you think so?

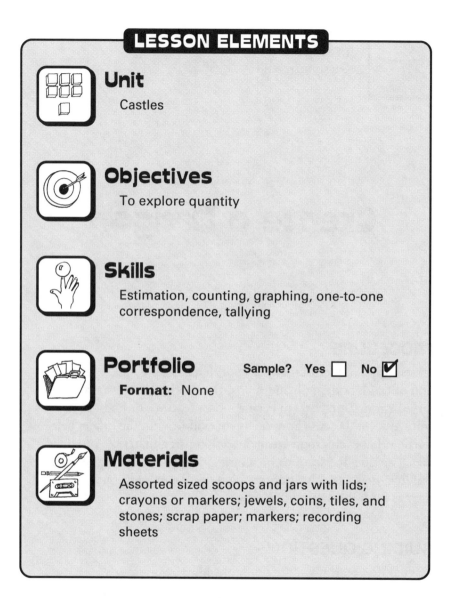

LESSON ELEMENTS

Unit
Castles

Objectives
To explore quantity

Skills
Estimation, counting, graphing, one-to-one correspondence, tallying

Portfolio
Format: None

Sample? Yes ☐ No ☑

Materials
Assorted sized scoops and jars with lids; crayons or markers; jewels, coins, tiles, and stones; scrap paper; markers; recording sheets

COMMENTS

Place a variety of materials in the math area for children to explore further.

Intelligence
Spatial/Artistic

Create a Dragon

PROCEDURE

Present dragon pictures and discuss shape, size, detail, and proportion of head, body, tail, and limbs. Divide children into groups of three or four and let them decide which features or body parts they will work on. Discuss how each part will fit with the others before starting. Let each group create a section using materials provided, then assemble the sections on a large piece of butcher paper. Let children view assembled dragon and decide on additional features such as neck, background, fire.

GUIDING QUESTIONS

- What do you think a dragon looks like?
- What features does a dragon's body have?
- How would a dragon's feet look? Would you paint or decorate your section first? Why?

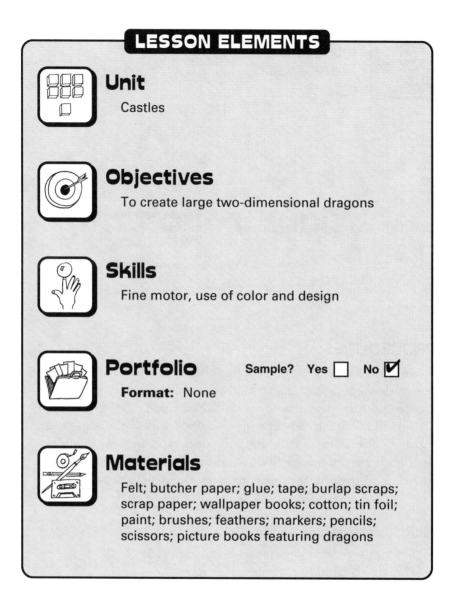

LESSON ELEMENTS

Unit
Castles

Objectives
To create large two-dimensional dragons

Skills
Fine motor, use of color and design

Portfolio
Sample? Yes ☐ No ☑

Format: None

Materials
Felt; butcher paper; glue; tape; burlap scraps; scrap paper; wallpaper books; cotton; tin foil; paint; brushes; feathers; markers; pencils; scissors; picture books featuring dragons

COMMENTS

Discuss the project as a whole group first. Let children make suggestions for how to plan the design and use the materials.

Intelligence
Spatial/Artistic

Clay Dragons

PROCEDURE

Provide pictures of dragons and let children describe features and details they notice. Let children make suggestions for how to use clay to create the dragons. Give each child a ball of clay. Let children manipulate the clay, making discoveries about its properties. Encourage children to share their discoveries. Notice how children use the clay and point out techniques such as rolling, pinching, pulling, and twisting for others to try with their clay.

GUIDING QUESTIONS

- How can you make the clay easier to manipulate?
- What do you notice as you use this clay?
- What techniques can you use to make a dragon with your clay?

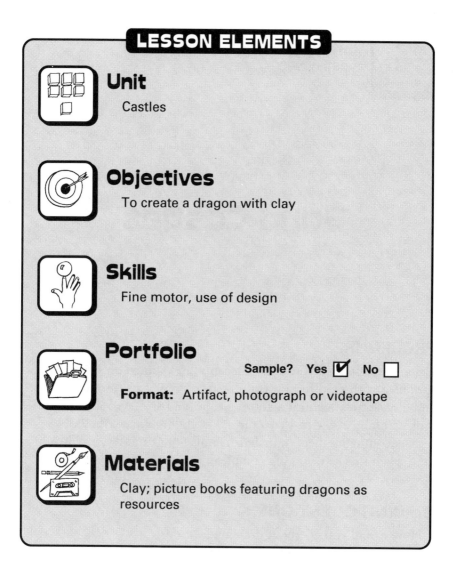

LESSON ELEMENTS

Unit
Castles

Objectives
To create a dragon with clay

Skills
Fine motor, use of design

Portfolio
Sample? Yes ☑ No ☐

Format: Artifact, photograph or videotape

Materials
Clay; picture books featuring dragons as resources

COMMENTS

Let all children share their finished dragons with the group. Let the group decide which dragons to save to accompany a castle display. Ask them to explain their choices.

Intelligence
Spatial/Artistic

Sand Castles

PROCEDURE

Demonstrate how a glue and water mixture painted on paper can be sprinkled with sand for a textured effect. Present pictures of castles and discuss architectural features, shape, and size. Ask children to look carefully at the castle pictures. Let children make their drawings, encouraging them to include details noted and discussed. Add sand when the drawings are complete.

GUIDING QUESTIONS

- How would you go about drawing a castle?
- What architectural features are important to include in your castle drawing?
- How could you use the sand and glue technique with your castle drawing?

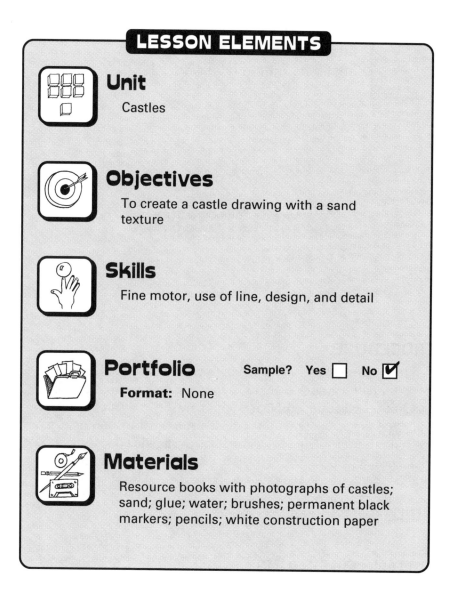

LESSON ELEMENTS

Unit
Castles

Objectives
To create a castle drawing with a sand texture

Skills
Fine motor, use of line, design, and detail

Portfolio
Format: None

Sample? Yes ☐ No ☑

Materials
Resource books with photographs of castles; sand; glue; water; brushes; permanent black markers; pencils; white construction paper

COMMENTS

Allow free exploration with the glue and water mixture in the art center. Provide other materials for adding texture to children's creations.

Intelligence
Inter- and Intrapersonal/Social

The Dragon

PROCEDURE

Tell the children that you are going to be reading a book in which there is a problem. Ask them to be thinking about who the main character is, what the problem is, and how the problem is solved while you are reading the story. Read a story that focuses on exploring and problem-solving behaviors such as showing off, being frightened, and being left out. Discuss the character, the problem, and the solution with the children. Have the children explore their personal experiences with showing off, being frightened, or being left out.

GUIDING QUESTIONS

- Why do you suppose some people show off?
- What do people do when they feel sad?
- How do you feel when people show off in front of you?
- What do you do when you feel sad?
- If you make a mistake and turn your friends against you, what can you do to change their dislike?

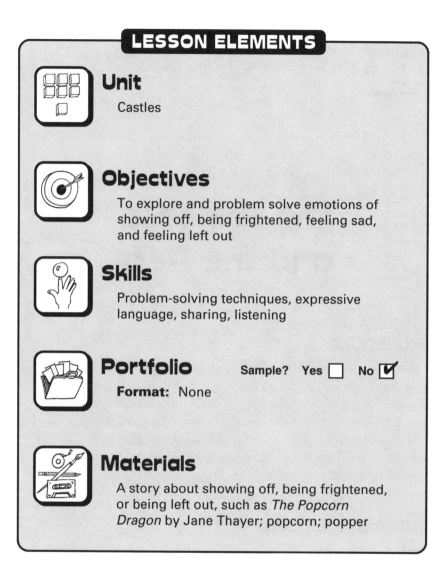

LESSON ELEMENTS

Unit
Castles

Objectives
To explore and problem solve emotions of showing off, being frightened, feeling sad, and feeling left out

Skills
Problem-solving techniques, expressive language, sharing, listening

Portfolio
Sample? Yes ☐ No ☑
Format: None

Materials
A story about showing off, being frightened, or being left out, such as *The Popcorn Dragon* by Jane Thayer; popcorn; popper

COMMENTS
To close the lesson, share popcorn as a sign of friendship.

Intelligence
Inter- and Intrapersonal/Social

The Princess and the Pea

PROCEDURE

The teacher tells the fairy tale, *The Princess and the Pea,* focusing on personality traits—noisy, clumsy, greedy, and unable to dance. Discuss the sequence of the story and the different personalities. Problem solve strategies for each princess. Make props available so that children can dramatize the story and/or the character traits of the princesses. Let each child or small group of children chose the parts they would like to dramatize.

GUIDING QUESTIONS

- What do you think the princess could have done to change her clumsiness?
- What can people change about themselves?
- What is not possible for people to change about themselves?
- Is there anything that you would like to change about yourself?
- What words would you use to describe your personality?

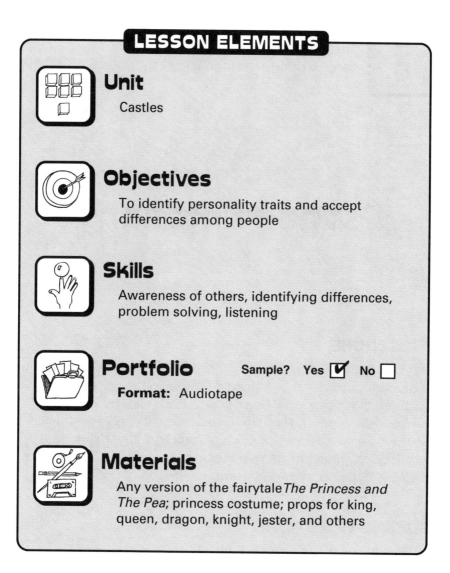

LESSON ELEMENTS

Unit
Castles

Objectives
To identify personality traits and accept differences among people

Skills
Awareness of others, identifying differences, problem solving, listening

Portfolio
Sample? Yes ☑ No ☐

Format: Audiotape

Materials
Any version of the fairytale *The Princess and The Pea*; princess costume; props for king, queen, dragon, knight, jester, and others

COMMENTS

To enhance the story and its magical qualities, the teacher may want to dress in a costume.

Intelligence
Inter- and Intrapersonal/Social

Dragon Emotions

PROCEDURE

Display pictures of dragons. In a large group brainstorm, explore, and record emotions of each dragon exhibited in the pictures (e.g., mean, frightened, sad, lonely, friendly). Divide children into small groups (three or four). Have each group use a variety of art supplies to create a certain type of dragon (e.g., sad, friendly). Upon completion, let each group present their pictures to the class, tell what their dragon is feeling, and why they think the dragon feels that way.

GUIDING QUESTIONS

- What do you notice about this picture of a dragon?
- What makes this dragon look mean?
- How could the dragon be changed to look friendly?
- What do you think the dragon would sound like?
- How do you think the dragon would move?

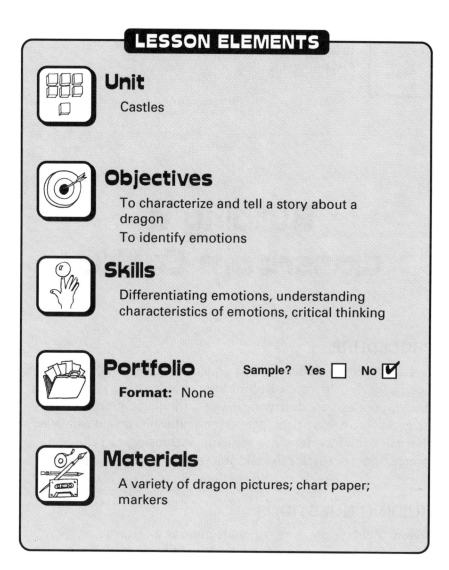

LESSON ELEMENTS

Unit
Castles

Objectives
To characterize and tell a story about a dragon
To identify emotions

Skills
Differentiating emotions, understanding characteristics of emotions, critical thinking

Portfolio
Sample? Yes ☐ No ☑
Format: None

Materials
A variety of dragon pictures; chart paper; markers

COMMENTS

Label each dragon picture with its emotion. Make these pictures available in the social center where children choose a picture and then act out the emotion for their peers to guess.

Intelligence
Spatial/Assembly

Building a Classroom Castle

PROCEDURE

Present materials and let children decide how to proceed in building a castle for the classroom. Record their ideas on chart paper and let small groups execute different parts of the building process. Different groups may make flags, plan crenelated walls, design windows, plan a drawbridge, etc. When the castle is completed let children sponge paint the surface to make it look like stone.

GUIDING QUESTIONS

- How could we use these materials to make a castle we can play in?
- How can these books help us?
- What features do you think our castle should have?
- How could we construct those features?

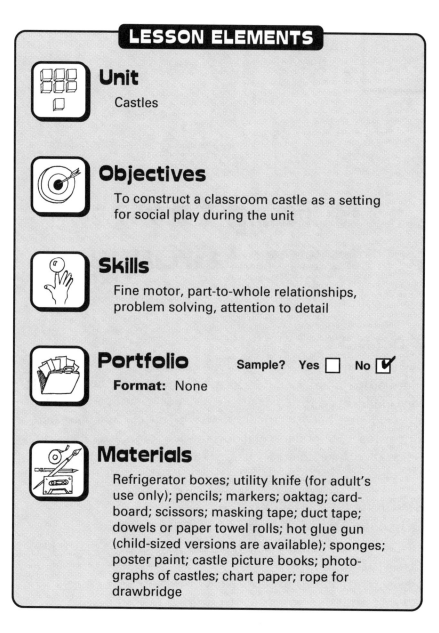

LESSON ELEMENTS

Unit
Castles

Objectives
To construct a classroom castle as a setting for social play during the unit

Skills
Fine motor, part-to-whole relationships, problem solving, attention to detail

Portfolio
Format: None

Sample? Yes ☐ No ☑

Materials
Refrigerator boxes; utility knife (for adult's use only); pencils; markers; oaktag; cardboard; scissors; masking tape; duct tape; dowels or paper towel rolls; hot glue gun (child-sized versions are available); sponges; poster paint; castle picture books; photographs of castles; chart paper; rope for drawbridge

COMMENTS
Let children dress up in costumes and provide props for exploring creative dramatic plays in the castle.

Intelligence
Spatial/Assembly

Building Castles
in Small Groups

PROCEDURE

Children work in small groups of three or four. Present each group
with a different problem. For example: How can you build a castle
with a tall narrow tower? many steps? a double wall? Allow time
for exploration and let each group view all the constructions and
then discuss each problem and how it was approached by the group.
Let children ask each other questions and suggest multiple solutions
to problems.

GUIDING QUESTIONS

- How will you use your materials to make a moat? a drawbridge?
  crenelated walls?
- How were you able to create a tall castle?
- Was it hard or easy to make steps? Why?

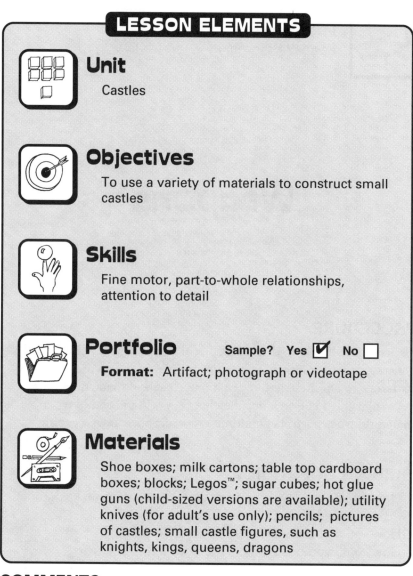

LESSON ELEMENTS

Unit
Castles

Objectives
To use a variety of materials to construct small castles

Skills
Fine motor, part-to-whole relationships, attention to detail

Portfolio
Sample? Yes ☑ No ☐
Format: Artifact; photograph or videotape

Materials
Shoe boxes; milk cartons; table top cardboard boxes; blocks; Legos™; sugar cubes; hot glue guns (child-sized versions are available); utility knives (for adult's use only); pencils; pictures of castles; small castle figures, such as knights, kings, queens, dragons

COMMENTS

Materials are so varied that children may want to have multiple building experiences. Leave materials in the assembly center for more exploration during free choice times. You may want to enlist the aid of parents or older children to assist with this project.

HOMEWORK

Create a castle at home.

243

Intelligence
Spatial/Assembly

Weapons

PROCEDURE

Use resource books to discuss medieval weaponry. Let children generate ideas for attaching handles to shields and swords. Present materials to children, letting them name each. Provide unfamiliar vocabulary. Let children decide what they will make and what materials are needed. Let children construct their own weapons.

GUIDING QUESTIONS

- How do you think we could use these materials to make the weapons knights used?
- How could you use this paper towel tube?
- How could you be sure the weapon wouldn't fall apart?

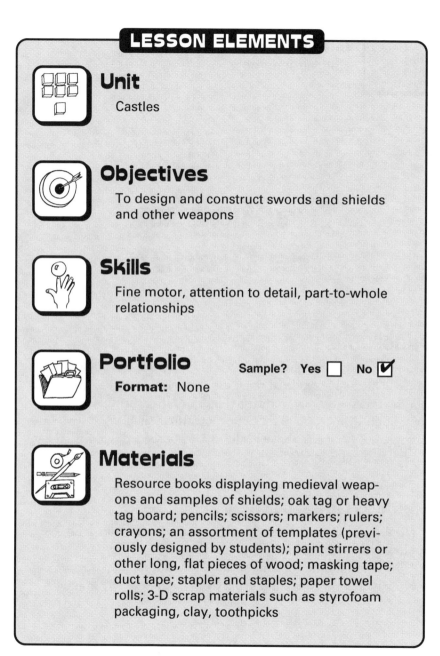

LESSON ELEMENTS

Unit
Castles

Objectives
To design and construct swords and shields and other weapons

Skills
Fine motor, attention to detail, part-to-whole relationships

Portfolio
Format: None

Sample? Yes ☐   No ☑

Materials
Resource books displaying medieval weapons and samples of shields; oak tag or heavy tag board; pencils; scissors; markers; rulers; crayons; an assortment of templates (previously designed by students); paint stirrers or other long, flat pieces of wood; masking tape; duct tape; stapler and staples; paper towel rolls; 3-D scrap materials such as styrofoam packaging, clay, toothpicks

COMMENTS

Wood scraps, hammers, and nails may be used as well. Save these weapons for the "Tournament of Knights" (Lesson 102).

Intelligence
Bodily-Kinesthetic

The King and the Dragon

PROCEDURE

Read or tell the dragon tale. Tell children to find their own space for movement. As the children retell the story with you, have them act out the events. Let children freely interpret the story action with their bodies while you point out observations such as, "I see a king lifting a heavy sword above his head," or "I see a dragon wagging his tail back and forth slowly."

GUIDING QUESTIONS

- How can you show a mean hungry dragon with your body?
- How would he walk?
- How do you think the king would look fighting the dragon?
- How would the king look being overpowered by the dragon?

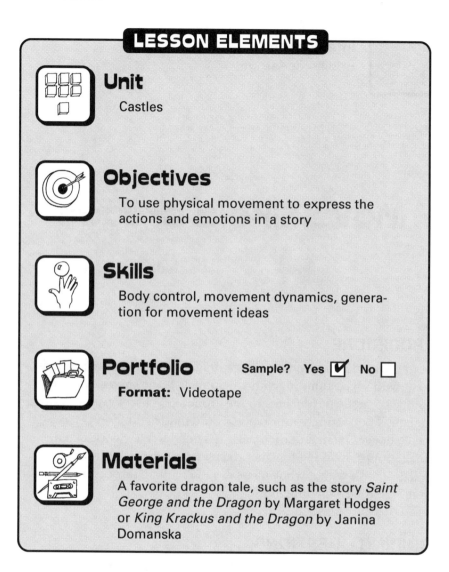

LESSON ELEMENTS

Unit
Castles

Objectives
To use physical movement to express the actions and emotions in a story

Skills
Body control, movement dynamics, generation for movement ideas

Portfolio
Sample? Yes ☑ No ☐

Format: Videotape

Materials
A favorite dragon tale, such as the story *Saint George and the Dragon* by Margaret Hodges or *King Krackus and the Dragon* by Janina Domanska

COMMENTS

If you notice a child making unusually well-executed or unique moves, point the moves out to the children. Suggest other children follow by saying, "Let's all try to move like (<u>name</u>) is doing."

Intelligence
Bodily-Kinesthetic

Move Like a Dragon

PROCEDURE

Brainstorm ideas for moving like a dragon and let children experiment with suggestions individually in their home spaces. Mention unique or subtle movements to the group, i.e. "I saw a slow floating dragon. Try floating your dragon." Add music and discuss movement changes related to each piece. Ask children to work in pairs or small groups, working together to create one dragon with their bodies. Finish with a whole-class dragon moving through the space to the children's favorite music.

GUIDING QUESTIONS

- How could you use your body to show the way a dragon moves?
- What parts will you move and how will you move them?
- How would a ferocious dragon move differently from a gentle, shy dragon?

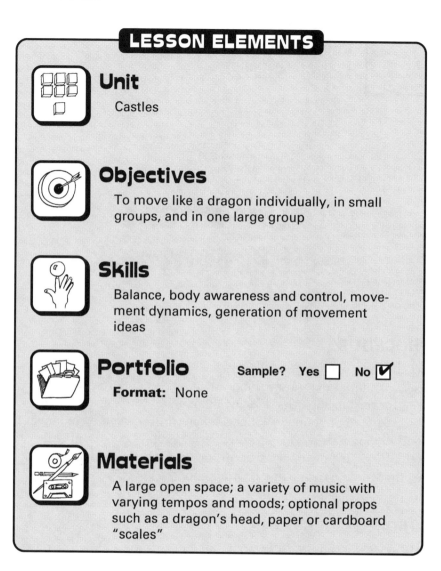

LESSON ELEMENTS

Unit
Castles

Objectives
To move like a dragon individually, in small groups, and in one large group

Skills
Balance, body awareness and control, movement dynamics, generation of movement ideas

Portfolio
Format: None

Sample? Yes ☐ No ☑

Materials
A large open space; a variety of music with varying tempos and moods; optional props such as a dragon's head, paper or cardboard "scales"

COMMENTS

Let children name other characters from the castle unit (such as king, princess, and court jester) and generate ways to move as these characters.

Intelligence
Bodily-Kinesthetic

Tournament of Knights

PROCEDURE

Let children practice using their swords and shields in their home space. Point out that safety is important and let children determine rules for the mock battles. Discuss the years of training and discipline required to become a knight. Re-enact the ceremony of knighthood so that each child is knighted by a "king." Let pairs of children engage in a mock battle according to the rules children have determined with each pair performing for the court.

GUIDING QUESTIONS

- How do you suppose a knight would move wearing heavy armor?
- Can you show how you would lunge with your sword and protect yourself with your shield?
- How can you pretend to fight but be sure no one is hurt?

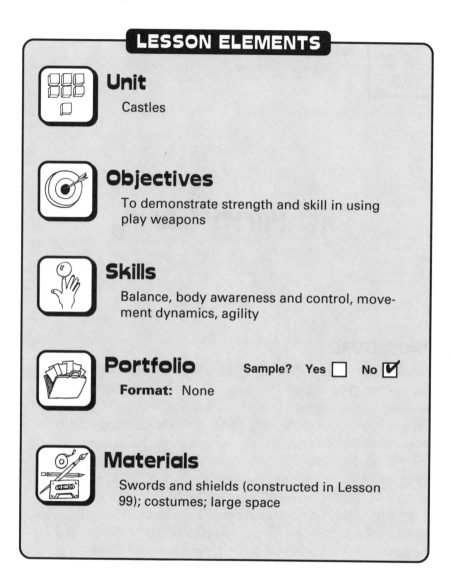

LESSON ELEMENTS

Unit
Castles

Objectives
To demonstrate strength and skill in using play weapons

Skills
Balance, body awareness and control, movement dynamics, agility

Portfolio
Sample? Yes ☐ No ☑
Format: None

Materials
Swords and shields (constructed in Lesson 99); costumes; large space

COMMENTS

A procession complete with pageantry may follow this activity.

HOMEWORK

Create a costume at home to wear in the procession.

Intelligence
Musical

Old King Glory

PROCEDURE

Part I—Familiarize children with the song "Old King Glory."
Choose one child to play Old King Glory. She or he should stand on
the outside of a large circle of children who are holding hands. As
the whole group sings the song and rotates clockwise, the King
moves in the opposite direction and taps three children as the words
"first," "second," and "third" are sung. The child tapped on the
word "third" leaves the circle and follows the King. Repeat the song
until all the children are following the King.

Part II—All children sit in a circle. The children brainstorm the
obstacles and terrain the King encounters on his way to the top of
the mountain. Using their voices, they create sound effects to go
with the list. Tell a story including all of the words brainstormed
and ask children to join in with their sound effects.

GUIDING QUESTIONS

- What obstacles do you think Old King Glory might have to ride
  over with his horse to get to the top of the mountain?
- How do you think the horse's hooves would sound running over
  (type of obstacle or terrain)?

252

UNIT: CASTLES

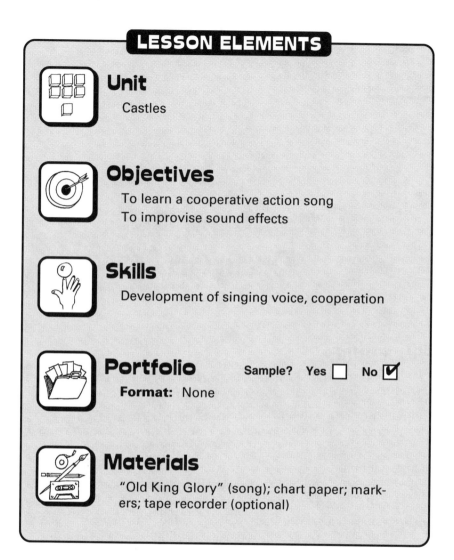

LESSON ELEMENTS

Unit
Castles

Objectives
To learn a cooperative action song
To improvise sound effects

Skills
Development of singing voice, cooperation

Portfolio
Format: None   Sample? Yes ☐ No ☑

Materials
"Old King Glory" (song); chart paper; markers; tape recorder (optional)

COMMENTS

In the music center, children gathered in small groups tell favorite stories adding sound effects. After they practice, they will record and present these stories to classmates.

253

Intelligence
Musical

The Generous Dragon

PROCEDURE

Create a story with the children in which a dragon is searching for his lost gold. Let children brainstorm a list of five to ten characters who will join the dragon in his search. Let children invent a unique way for the dragon and his friends to find the gold. Each character should go home with some of the gold the dragon has generously given away in appreciation.

Explain to the children that they will create a crescendo to the story by adding instruments to the beat of the dragon's footsteps. Let children suggest a way to keep the beat as the dragon walks (such as slapping thighs). Discuss the sequence of characters who join the dragon and ask children to choose an instrument to represent each character. Let children practice keeping the beat with their body, then add instruments one at a time until all children are playing and/or keeping the beat. Delete instruments as each character departs to go home.

Practice, then retell the story building the crescendo. Use repetitive language such as "Along came a _____ who said _____" to allow children to join in the storytelling. (The crescendo should enhance the excitement of finally finding the gold.)

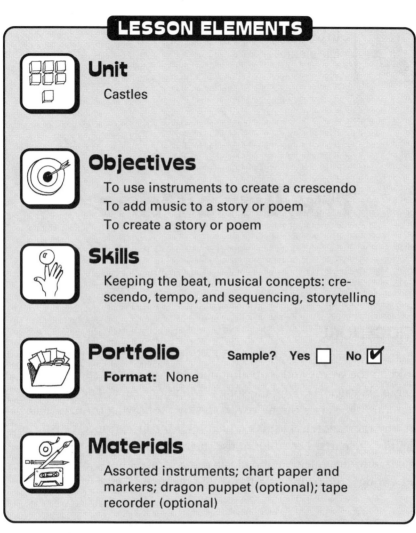

LESSON ELEMENTS

Unit
Castles

Objectives
To use instruments to create a crescendo
To add music to a story or poem
To create a story or poem

Skills
Keeping the beat, musical concepts: crescendo, tempo, and sequencing, storytelling

Portfolio
Sample? Yes ☐ No ☑
Format: None

Materials
Assorted instruments; chart paper and markers; dragon puppet (optional); tape recorder (optional)

GUIDING QUESTIONS
- How can we create the dragon's footsteps as he walks along?
- What instrument makes a sound that reminds you of this character?

COMMENTS
Make pictures of each character for young children. After the children know the story well, ask them to "tell" the story without using words. They may use puppets or pictures and instruments only.

Intelligence
Musical

The Little Prince

PROCEDURE

Begin by humming the tune to "The Little Prince." Teach the children the words and let them point out the days of the week on their class calendar. Sing the song through one time. The second time vary the verses (high, low, fast, slow) following changes generated by the children. Display a picture of the little prince's castle and identify the parts. Let children use their voices to invent sounds for the drawbridge opening and closing, the prince's horse crossing the drawbridge, the trumpets announcing the arrival, etc.

GUIDING QUESTIONS

- What do you notice that stays the same in each verse? is different in each verse?
- How can you use your voice to change the song?

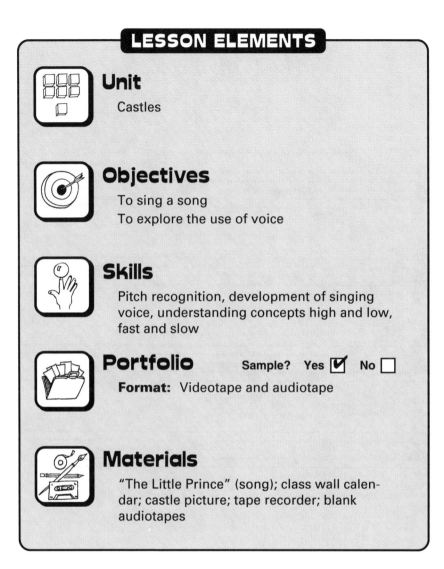

LESSON ELEMENTS

Unit
Castles

Objectives
To sing a song
To explore the use of voice

Skills
Pitch recognition, development of singing voice, understanding concepts high and low, fast and slow

Portfolio   Sample? Yes ☑ No ☐
Format: Videotape and audiotape

Materials
"The Little Prince" (song); class wall calendar; castle picture; tape recorder; blank audiotapes

COMMENTS

Make a tape recorder and blank tapes available at the music center for small groups of children to record and listen to their sound effects.

The Little Prince

English Words by B. L. and E. C.   French Folk Song

The whole family goes visiting almost every day of the week.

1. Mon- day at   noon, there came The King and Queen and Prince, O,

Came   to   my   house   to   pay   a   call   on   me,   O,

But   since   I   was   a - way,   The   lit - tle Prince did   say,

"Tues - day   at   noon,   I   will   come   back   a -   gain."

2. Tuesday at noon, . . .   5. Friday at noon, . . .

3. Wednesday at noon, . . .   6. Saturday at noon, . . .
                                   . . . "Sunday at noon
4. Thursday at noon, . . .   I will not come again."

CASTLE UNIT BIBLIOGRAPHY

Aliki. (1983). *A Medieval Feast*. New York: HarperCollins.

Carle, E. (1991). *Dragons, Dragons and Other Creatures That Were*. New York: Putnam.

DePaola, T. (1980). *The Knight and the Dragon*. New York: Putnam.

Domanska, J. (1979). *King Krackus and the Dragon*. New York: Greenwillow.

Grimm, J., and Grimm, W. (1986). "The Frog Prince," *Complete Brothers Grimm Fairy Tales*. Avenal, N.J.: Outlet Books.

Grimm, J., and Grimm, W. (1989). "Cinderella," *Children's Classics: Grimm's Fairy Tales*. New York: Simon & Schuster.

Grimm, J., and Grimm, W. (1989). "Rapunzel," *Children's Classics: Grimm's Fairy Tales*. New York: Simon & Schuster.

Grimm, J., and Grimm, W. (1989). "Rumplestiltskin," *Children's Classics: Grimm's Fairy Tales*. New York: Simon & Schuster.

Grahame, K. (1988). *The Reluctant Dragon*. New York: H. Holt & Co.

Hodges, M. (1990). *St. George and the Dragon*. New York: Little, Brown & Co.

Huck, C. (1989). *Princess Furball*. New York: Greenwillow.

Fraser, J., and Dreuter, K. (1987). "Old King Glory." *Discovering Orff*. New York: Schott.

Littledale, F. (1969). *King Midas and the Golden Touch*. New York: Random House.

Macaulay, D. (1982). *Castle*. New York: Houghton Mifflin.

Peet, B. (1984). *Cowardly Clyde*. New York: Houghton Mifflin.

Silver Burdett Company. (1971). "The Little Prince." *Making Music Your Own*. Morristown, N.Y.: Silver Burdett.

Stevens, J. (1982). *The Princess and the Pea*. New York: Holiday House.

Thayer, J. (1989). *The Popcorn Dragon*. New York: Morrow Jr. Books.

Wood, A. (1985). *King Bidgood's in the Bathtub*. New York: Hartcourt Brace & Co.

Index

There are
one-story intellects,
two-story intellects, and three-story
intellects with skylights. All fact collectors, who
have no aim beyond their facts, are one-story men. Two-story men
compare, reason, generalize, using the labors of the fact collectors as
well as their own. Three-story men idealize, imagine,
predict—their best illumination comes from
above, through the skylight.
—*Oliver Wendell*
Holmes

SkyLight
PROFESSIONAL DEVELOPMENT

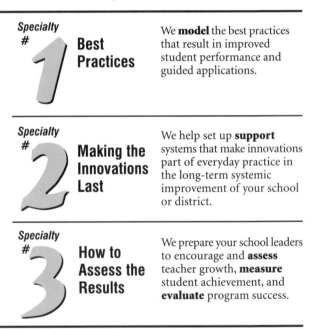